Teacher's Resource Guide

2
3

Reading and Writing for Today's Adults
Voyager

Advisers to the Series

Mary Dunn Siedow
Director
North Carolina Literacy Resource Center
Raleigh, NC

Linda Thistlethwaite
Associate Director
The Central Illinois Adult Education Service Center
Western Illinois University
Macomb, IL

New Readers Press

Contributing Writers

Book 2 Teacher's Notes: Cathy Niemet

Book 3 Teacher's Notes: Susan McShane

Voyager: Reading and Writing for Today's Adults™ Teacher's Resource Guide for Voyager 2 and 3
ISBN 1-56420-169-4
Copyright © 1999
New Readers Press
U.S. Publishing Division of Laubach Literacy International
Box 131, Syracuse, New York 13210-0131

Printed in the United States of America
9 8 7 6 5 4

Director of Acquisitions and Development: Christina Jagger
Content Editor: Mary Hutchison
Developer: Learning Unlimited, Oak Park, IL
Developmental Editor: Pamela Bliss
Cover Designer: Gerald Russell
Designer: Kimbrly Koennecke
Copy Editor: Jeanna H. Walsh
Artist/Illustrator: Linda Alden

Contents

Overview of the Series

Voyager: Reading and Writing for Today's Adults is a four-stage program that utilizes contemporary content and instructional approaches to teach the reading, writing, critical thinking, and communication skills that adults need in today's world. It takes students from the beginning stages of reading and writing through the ninth-grade level.

The *Voyager* series consists of nine student books, nine workbooks, four teacher's resource guides, and a placement tool.

▶ Key Features and Benefits

1. ***Voyager* integrates contemporary content and instructional approaches with the best elements from traditional instruction and practice.** In the early books, phonics and other word recognition strategies are combined with reading comprehension instruction. Later books emphasize comprehension and meaning. Instruction in the writing process is combined with instruction in spelling, capitalization, punctuation, grammar, usage, and sentence structure. This balanced approach results in a solid, effective program.

2. **Each lesson integrates reading, writing, listening, speaking, and thinking skills.** Research has shown that literacy development is enhanced when students have the opportunity to apply all these skills to a single topic. Activities and skill-building exercises in *Voyager* are related to the topic of the reading selection, the core of the lesson.

3. ***Voyager* is theme-based.** In *Foundation Book,* each lesson has a theme. The other eight student books are divided into four units, each with its own theme. This theme-based approach encourages students to delve into a topic using a variety of approaches. As students complete the reading, writing, and thinking activities in a unit, they have opportunities to examine the common concepts and issues associated with that unit's theme.

4. **Students work with authentic reading selections and writing assignments—practical,** informational, and literary. *Voyager* draws from a combination of high-quality literature, information-rich articles, adult student writings, and the types of forms, documents, and graphic material adults commonly encounter. Working with these materials, students achieve success at both academic and everyday reading and writing activities.

5. **Activities in *Voyager* give students opportunities to work both independently and collaboratively.** Students complete some activities by themselves. In other activities, students participate in discussions, group problem solving, and so on. These varied ways of working reflect daily life.

6. ***Voyager* can be successfully used in a variety of settings.** *Voyager* can be used in large- or small-group instructional programs, in one-on-one tutorial situations, and independently for self-study in an individualized or learning lab program. This flexible instructional format meets the needs of a wide variety of programs.

7. ***Voyager* provides additional support for both students and teachers.** Workbooks, to be used independently by students, are filled with exercises that give them extra practice with the major skills taught in the lessons. Teacher's resource guides provide valuable additional background information, teaching ideas, and photocopy masters (PCMs). These support materials save time by helping teachers create lesson plans and reinforcement materials.

▶ A Closer Look at *Voyager* Components

▶ **Nine student books** form the instructional core of the *Voyager* program.

▶ **Nine workbooks,** one for each student book, provide students with extra skills practice.

▶ **Four teacher's resource guides,** one for each stage, contain a general overview and orientation to each stage, lesson-by-lesson teacher's notes and extension activities for the student books, and PCMs for both instruction and assessment.

▶ **The placement tool** helps teachers place students in the appropriate *Voyager* student book.

The Four Stages

The *Voyager* series is a four-stage program. Each stage of *Voyager* reflects a separate stage of reading and writing development. Thus, each stage has its own emphasis and design. The four stages are

1. **Learning to Read** (Reading levels 0.5–2.5) Emphasis at this stage is on short reading selections containing common words; phonics instruction; and writing, speaking, and listening activities to teach basic skills and build confidence.

2. **The Emerging Reader** (Reading levels 2.0–4.5) Emphasis at this stage is on literary and informational reading selections; phonics and other word recognition strategies; comprehension and critical thinking strategies; and writing, speaking, and listening skills.

3. **Reading to Learn** (Reading levels 4.0–7.5) Emphasis at this stage is on expanding students' reading, thinking, writing, and oral communication skills, using reading materials typically found at home, at work, at school, and in the community.

4. **Reading for Work and Life** (Reading levels 7.0–9.5) Emphasis at this stage is on having students learn and apply reading, thinking, writing, and oral communications skills through themes and readings that are work- and life-oriented.

Components of the *Voyager* Series

Stages	Student Books (96 – 176 pages)	Reading Levels	Workbooks (48 pages each)	Teacher's Resource Guides
Learning to Read	Voyager Foundation Book (96 pages)	0.5 – 1.5	Voyager Foundation Workbook	Teacher's Resource Guide for Foundation Book and Voyager 1 (80 pages)
	Voyager 1 (128 pages)	1.0 – 2.5	Voyager 1 Workbook	
The Emerging Reader	Voyager 2 (128 pages)	2.0 – 3.5	Voyager 2 Workbook	Teacher's Resource Guide for Voyager 2 and 3 (80 pages)
	Voyager 3 (128 pages)	3.0 – 4.5	Voyager 3 Workbook	
Reading to Learn	Voyager 4 (160 pages)	4.0 – 5.5	Voyager 4 Workbook	Teacher's Resource Guide for Voyager 4 – 6 (96 pages)
	Voyager 5 (160 pages)	5.0 – 6.5	Voyager 5 Workbook	
	Voyager 6 (160 pages)	6.0 – 7.5	Voyager 6 Workbook	
Reading for Work and Life	Voyager 7 (176 pages)	7.0 – 8.5	Voyager 7 Workbook	Teacher's Resource Guide for Voyager 7 and 8 (80 pages)
	Voyager 8 (176 pages)	8.0 – 9.5	Voyager 8 Workbook	

▶ A Closer Look at the Student Books

Voyager contains nine student books.

Foundation Book

The first book is *Foundation Book*. This book has 28 lessons divided into five units. Units 1–3 contain 18 lessons and introduce the sounds and names of single consonants. Unit 4 contains five lessons that introduce the five vowels and the short vowel sounds in a word-family context. Unit 5 contains five lessons introducing common initial consonant blends.

The activities in each lesson give students opportunities to generate words containing the target letters and sounds, and to read and write sentences or stories that contain words with those letters and sounds. The lessons also include activities to build listening, speaking, and critical-thinking skills.

Student Books 1–8

▷ **Units:** Student books 1–8 are each divided into four units organized around themes relevant to adult life, such as Hopes and Dreams, Express Yourself, On the Job, and Resolving Conflict. Each unit contains three lessons in which students explore different aspects of the theme while working with activities that integrate reading, writing, listening, speaking, and thinking skills.

Each unit ends with (1) a one-page Writing Skills Mini-Lesson that teaches a specific writing skill, such as capitalization, and (2) a cumulative unit review that covers the main skills taught in the unit.

▶ **Lessons:** Lessons in student books 1–8 contain the following features.

Pre-Reading Activities: Each lesson begins with a pre-reading activity designed to activate student interest and prior knowledge, or to teach information needed to understand the reading at the heart of the lesson.

Reading Selections: Over the course of the series, students are exposed to a wide variety of authentic, high-quality reading selections. The readings are a rich mixture of short stories; poetry; drama; essays; adult student writings; informational pieces; and common documents, forms, and graphics.

Post-Reading Activities: Through activities related to the reading selection and the unit's theme, students develop their vocabulary, comprehension, and higher-order thinking skills; build their writing competence; and work to master common documents, forms, and graphics. The blend of these features depends on the level of the book.

▶ **Assessment:** Each book begins with a Skills Preview and ends with a cumulative Skills Review. Books 1–6 also contain student self-assessments to use before beginning and after completing each book.

▶ **Answer Key and Reference Handbook:** Students can find an answer key and a reference handbook at the back of each book.

The diagram below shows the organization of Books 1–8.

Organization of *Voyager* Books 1-8

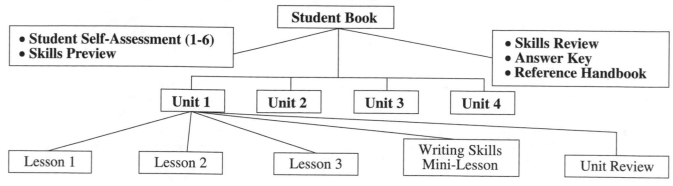

▶ A Closer Look at Assessment

Assessment in *Voyager* is based on these principles:

1. **Assessment should inform instruction.** Assessment can monitor a student's progress, provide feedback and a framework for remediation, and determine mastery.

2. **Assessment should allow learners to express expectations and evaluate progress.** Specific instruments can help students express their goals and needs and evaluate what they have learned.

3. **Assessment should allow for measurement and documentation of a student's progress and educational gains.** Such documentation is essential for students, teachers, and schools.

Series Assessment Tools

This program provides these assessment tools:

- The **Placement Tool** will help you to place a student in the appropriate *Voyager* student book.
- **Student Interest Inventories** in Books 1–3 and **Student Self-Assessments** in Books 4–6 let students evaluate their level of activity and proficiency with various reading and writing tasks.
- The **Skills Preview** in each student book tests students' proficiency with the reading and writing tasks to be covered in the book.
- **Unit Reviews** test the key skills in the unit.
- The **Skills Review** in each student book tests the key reading and writing skills taught in the entire book.

Alternative Assessment Tools

You can utilize any of the following alternative assessment instruments with *Voyager.*

▶ Writing

Dialogue Journals: A student writes observations and ideas in a journal on an ongoing basis, and the teacher responds in the journal (see page 19).

Writing Portfolios: These are collections of student writings (see page 20).

▶ Personal Progress Portfolios

Working Folders: Students date and keep all their works-in-progress and finished work in their working folders. They also keep their "Student Progress Tracking Sheets" in this folder.

Progress Portfolios: Progress Portfolios let students demonstrate progress over time. PCMs have instructions for helping *Voyager* students evaluate the material in their working folders and assemble Progress Portfolios.

▶ Evaluation

Student conferences allow you to evaluate a student's portfolio. These conferences should help students to see their progress as well as show them areas that need improvement. A PCM is provided as a guide for conducting these conferences.

Main Purposes of Voyager Assessment Tools

	Inform Instructor	Empower Learner	Measure Progress
Series Assessments			
Placement Tool	X		
Student Interest Inventory		X	X
Skills Preview	X	X	X
Unit Review	X	X	X
Skills Review	X	X	X
Alternative Assessments			
Dialogue Journal	X	X	
Writing Portfolio	X	X	X
Personal Progress Portfolio	X	X	X

Voyager 2 Scope and Sequence

Unit	Part of Unit	Reading Selection	Genre	Reading Strategy
Unit 1: Family Ties	Lesson 1	Family Is Family	Story	Imagine
	Lesson 2	To My Son	Letter	Retell
	Lesson 3	The Quarrel	Poetry	Use prior experience
	Writing Skills Mini-Lesson			
	Unit 1 Review	Grandma Pat	Prose	
Unit 2: Life Goes On	Lesson 4	Saying Good-bye	Story	Imagine
	Lesson 5	Lament	Poetry	Use prior knowledge
	Lesson 6	Life in the Hearing World	Biography	Retell
	Writing Skills Mini-Lesson			
	Unit 2 Review	Where There Is a Will There Is a Way	Autobiographical account	
Unit 3: New Beginnings	Lesson 7	Follow the Drinking Gourd	Song	Use prior knowledge
	Lesson 8	Al's Journal	Journal	Imagine
	Lesson 9	A New World	Autobiographical account	Retell
	Writing Skills Mini-Lesson			
	Unit 3 Review	The Empty Nest	Story	
Unit 4: Celebrate Differences	Lesson 10	Neighborly Celebrations	Story	Use prior experience
	Lesson 11	Celebrate an American Life	Biography	Use prior knowledge
	Lesson 12	Manhattan *and* You've Got to Be Carefully Taught	Poetry	Use prior knowledge
	Writing Skills Mini-Lesson			
	Unit 4 Review	In a Strange City	Story	

Reading and Thinking Skill	Writing	Speaking and Listening	Word Work	TRG pages	Workbook pages
Understand plot	Write a sequence of events	Retell	The vowel combinations *ie* and *ei*	22 – 23	4 – 5
Understand the main idea and details	Write a letter	Discussion	The letter combinations *ow* and *ou*	23 – 24	6 – 7
Identify rhythm and rhyme	Write a poem	Oral reading		24 – 25	8
	Adding endings that start with a vowel			25	9 – 10
				26	11 – 13
Understand character	Write a note	Discussion	Context clues	27 – 28	14 – 15
Understand the use of repetition	Write a poem	Oral reading		29 – 30	16
Make inferences	Write a letter	Retell	Context clues	30 – 31	17 – 18
	Using capital letters			31	19 – 20
				31	21 – 23
Make inferences	Write about a song	Oral reading		32 – 33	24
Understand the main idea and details	Write a journal entry	Discussion	Compound words	33 – 34	25 – 26
Make inferences	Write an interview	Interview	Prefixes and roots	34 – 36	27 – 28
	Writing sentences			36	29 – 30
				36	31 – 33
Understand plot and character	Write a description	Retell	Suffixes *-ful, -less, -able, -or*	37 – 38	34 – 35
Make inferences	Write your autobiography	Discussion	The suffix *-ion*	38 – 39	36 – 37
Identify rhyme, rhythm, and repetition	Write a poem	Oral reading/ discussion		39 – 40	38
	Compound sentences			40 – 41	39 – 40
				41	41 – 43

Voyager 3 Scope and Sequence

Unit	Part of Unit	Reading Selection	Genre	Reading Strategy
Unit 1: Great Expectations	Lesson 1	It Could Be a Wonderful World	Song	Use prior experience
	Lesson 2	The New Boss	Story	Predict
	Lesson 3	Shaq Measures Up	Biography	Empathize
	Writing Skills Mini-Lesson			
	Unit 1 Review	High Hopes	Story	
Unit 2: Across Generations	Lesson 4	Lineage	Poetry	Use prior experience
	Lesson 5	A Mother's Gift	Journal	Predict
	Lesson 6	Suspect	Story	Empathize
	Writing Skills Mini-Lesson			
	Unit 2 Review	Nothing New	Story	
Unit 3: Voices for Justice	Lesson 7	A Safe Place	Story	Predict
	Lesson 8	Voice of a People	Biography	Use prior knowledge
	Lesson 9	Let Me Be a Free Man	Speech	Empathize
	Writing Skills Mini-Lesson			
	Unit 3 Review	Defending the Poor	Prose	
Unit 4: Express Yourself	Lesson 10	Marian Anderson: A Tribute	Review	Use prior knowledge
	Lesson 11	A Soldier's Story	Story	Predict
	Lesson 12	Arthur	Poetry	Use prior experience
	Writing Skills Mini-Lesson			
	Unit 4 Review	A Letter to the Editor	Letter	

Reading and Thinking Skill	Writing	Speaking and Listening	Word Work	TRG pages	Workbook pages
Find the theme	Write a song	Oral reading		43 – 44	4
Understand the plot	Write a story	Discussion	Context clues	44 – 45	5 – 6
Find the main idea and details	Write a paragraph	Interview	Recognizing words	45 – 47	7 – 8
	Compound sentences			47	9 – 10
				47	11 – 13
Find the theme	Write a poem	Oral reading		48 – 49	14
Draw conclusions	Write a journal entry	Discussion	Prefixes and roots	49 – 51	15 – 16
Understand character	Describe a character	Retell	Prefixes, roots, and suffixes	51 – 52	17 – 18
	Complex sentences			52	19 – 20
				52	21 – 23
Identify setting	Describe a setting	Retell	Dividing words into syllables	53 – 55	24 – 25
Find the main idea and details	Write an interview	Interview	More dividing words into syllables	55 – 56	26 – 27
Identify viewpoint	Write your viewpoint	Discussion		56 – 57	28
	More on complex sentences			57	29 – 30
				57	31 – 33
Identify viewpoint	Write a review	Discussion	Review of dividing words into syllables	58 – 59	34 – 35
Understand character setting, and plot	Write a story	Oral reading	Summary of word-recognition strategies	59 – 60	36 – 37
Make inferences	Write a letter	Discussion		60 – 61	38
	Fixing sentence fragments			61 – 62	39 – 40
				62	41 – 43

Overview of *Voyager 2* and *Voyager 3*

▶ Parts of the Books

Voyager 2 and *Voyager 3* are each divided into four theme-based units to give students a meaningful context for their reading, writing, thinking, listening, and speaking activities.

The Four Units

Below is a short explanation of the unit features in *Voyager 2* and *Voyager 3*. Detailed explanations and tips for teaching the lessons and mini-lessons are in the Teacher's Notes starting on page 21.

Unit Overviews The overview introduces the theme of the unit. The readings and activities throughout a unit are related to its theme.

Lessons Each unit has three lessons. Each lesson contains these features:

- **Learning Goals** a list of the main objectives of each lesson. Knowing the goals for study empowers students to take charge of the learning process.
- **Before You Read** a strategy to help students prepare for the reading selection. Students are encouraged to think about their own knowledge of or experience with the reading topic, or they are given essential background information.
- **Key Words** words in the lesson that students may not recognize or know the meaning of, presented in a meaningful context
- **Use the Strategy** a reminder, to help students apply the reading strategy
- **Reading** a story, poem, letter, article, biography, or journal entry relating to the unit's theme
- **After You Read** questions and activities to check students' comprehension of and reaction to the reading selection
- **Think About It** instruction and practice in a targeted reading and thinking skill
- **Write About It** instruction and guided practice in producing a piece of writing, such as a letter or a poem

- **Word Work** instruction and practice in word-attack strategies—phonics, context clues, and word analysis—to help students better decode and write words

Writing Skills Mini-Lessons Each unit has a one-page mini-lesson after the last lesson. The mini-lessons explore a particular issue of mechanics or sentence structure to help students master basic conventions of written English.

Unit Reviews The Unit Reviews recap the reading and writing activities in each unit. The writing process is introduced and practiced.

Before Starting the Units

Student Interest Inventory This assessment tool lets students evaluate their current level of activity and proficiency with a variety of everyday reading and writing tasks. You will need to work through it individually with students.

Skills Preview The Skills Preview helps you diagnose how well students read independently.

While Working through the Units

Answer Key The Answer Key provides answers to exercises in the lessons, Unit Reviews, and Writing Skills Mini-Lessons.

Reference Handbook This handbook contains
- **Writing Skills** a summary of the information in the mini-lessons
- **The Writing Process** an outline of the five stages of the writing process

After Working through the Units

Skills Review The Skills Review is a cumulative review of the skills taught in *Voyager 2* or *Voyager 3*. If students do well on the Skills Review, you should feel comfortable moving them on to the next *Voyager* book.

▶ How to Use *Voyager 2* and *Voyager 3*

You can use *Voyager 2* and *Voyager 3* for one-on-one or group instruction. The Teacher's Notes that start on page 21 will guide you through each lesson in these books. You may adapt these notes to fit your specific needs.

Before you begin working with *Voyager 2* or *Voyager 3*, read the "Suggestions for Teaching *Voyager 2* and *Voyager 3*" on page 15. This material gives insight into the special needs of adult emerging readers and writers. It suggests specific strategies that have proven to be successful with adult literacy students.

To begin your work, discuss students' educational goals with them. Describe ways in which you will be helping them reach those goals. Work through the assessment materials at the beginning of the book to assess students' skill levels and needs.

As you work through *Voyager 2* or *Voyager 3* with students, assess what material each student can do independently and on what type of material he or she needs guidance. Encourage as much independence as possible, but be careful not to frustrate students by having unrealistic expectations.

Adult students need a lot of feedback. Focus on the positive—what students have learned or accomplished. Keep in mind, however, that adult students can also detect insincere praise, so be positive, but truthful.

Working with a Range of Students in a Group Setting

If you are involved in group instruction, your students' literacy levels may vary. Students may range from those who are new to reading to those who need just a review before moving on. It is essential that you get to know your group members as individuals with very specific interests and skill levels.

Although students may be placed in a group based on their assessed reading level, you will find that adult students have diverse skills and skill levels. The following strategies can be used with a mixed-ability group:

- Work through the first unit with the entire class. If some students move quickly through the material on their own, let those students work ahead in a lesson independently, drawing them back in for whole-group discussions and peer review of writing assignments.
- Involve the more able students in peer tutoring. For instance, have students read to each other and review each other's writing and practice work.
- The more able students can do reinforcement and extension activities while the rest of the group finishes a lesson. They can complete the corresponding workbook pages independently or the extension activities suggested in the Teacher's Notes.

Using the Student Interest Inventory

Before starting, explain to students that they will fill in the left side of the chart now and the right side after finishing the book. Also point out that it will help you get to know the student better and will give the student a way to evaluate his or her progress over time.

Have the student try to read and fill in his or her educational goal independently. If necessary, read it aloud and fill in the student's dictated answer.

Then you or the student should read the central column. The student should check the appropriate answer for each item on the left side of the chart.

Using the Skills Preview

Work one-on-one with a student to complete the preview. Read the directions to each section aloud. Then have the student complete the section as independently as possible.

Use the Skills Preview Answers and the Skills Chart to get a sense of the student's comfort level with material taught in *Voyager 2* or *Voyager 3*. Discuss the results with the student.

If a student has great difficulty with the Skills Preview, consider using the previous *Voyager* book instead. Conversely, if a student has little or no difficulty, you can have the student complete the Skills Review. If this is also easily completed, consider using the next level *Voyager* book.

Working through the Lessons

The Teacher's Notes on pages 21–62 provide teaching suggestions for each lesson in *Voyager 2* and *Voyager 3*.

Working with the Reading Selections

The reading selection is the heart of each lesson. With any student or group of students, read the title aloud. Ask students to look at the picture. Ask what they think the reading will be about. Depending on class size, you can use the following strategies to help students better understand the reading:

▶ **One-on-one tutoring:** Skim the selection to determine whether you think the student will be able to read it independently or will need assistance.

- If you think the student can read the selection independently, have him or her read it aloud to you. If the student mispronounces or skips a word, let him or her continue to read, see that the sentence did not make sense, and correct the error. If the student does not self-correct after one or two sentences, wait until he or she has finished reading and then have the student reread the incorrect sentence.
- If you think the student will need assistance, try one of the assisted reading strategies described on page 17.

▶ **Group instruction:** Skim the selection and use one of these strategies, depending on the difficulty of the selection:

- If you think students will need assistance, try one of the assisted reading strategies described on page 17.
- Read the entire selection aloud to students. Then have students read it to themselves. Next, have volunteers each read a sentence or paragraph aloud to the class.

- Read the first paragraph aloud to students. Then have volunteers read the remaining paragraphs aloud. Finally, have students read the entire selection to themselves.

Using the Answer Key

Check students' answers as they complete an exercise or lesson. When students are able, let them check and correct their own work.

Using the Reference Handbook

Here are some tips:
- **Writing Skills** Have students refer to these pages whenever they are editing their writing.
- **The Writing Process** Refer students to this page when they do the writing portion of a unit review.

Using the Skills Review

Have students complete the review independently. Use the Skills Review Answers and Evaluation Charts to help students evaluate their performance. Read students' Write About It pieces and give them feedback on all parts of the writing process.

Discuss the review results with students. If a student struggled through or performed poorly on a section of the Skills Review, assess the problem area(s). You may want the student to review the lessons and/or units in which these areas are covered before moving them into the next *Voyager* book.

Finally, have students return to the Student Interest Inventory and fill out the right side of the chart. Discuss their progress and ongoing goals.

Suggestions for Teaching
Voyager 2 and *Voyager 3*

▶ Purpose of *Voyager 2* and *Voyager 3*

Voyager 2 and *Voyager 3* emphasize the key components of the reading and writing processes. Students engage in various prereading strategies, and postreading comprehension activities follow each reading. In addition, students practice such higher-order thinking skills as making inferences, identifying main idea and detail, and identifying plot and character traits, based on the reading selections. Students also follow the key stages of the writing process as they complete a writing activity related to the reading. Students develop their listening and speaking skills as they participate in oral activities in each lesson.

After successfully completing *Voyager 2* and *Voyager 3*, students will have learned to
- work through theme-based units
- apply word recognition strategies: context clues, word analysis, phonics, and syllabication
- use context clues to determine the meaning of unknown words
- use a variety of reading strategies and skills to improve comprehension
- apply the writing process to writing poems, letters, journal entries, paragraphs, and other pieces
- use written English conventions, such as capitalization, spelling, and writing complete sentences

▶ Characteristics of Adult Emerging Readers

When working with these materials, keep in mind the following characteristics common to adult learners.

Adult learners	As a teacher or tutor of adult learners you should
want and deserve respect but may fear school	• stress accomplishments • give frequent praise • emphasize existing skills
have a wealth of life experience	• emphasize how much students already can do • design some activities around students' interests and experiences
may feel insecure about using new skills	• provide many opportunities for practice • model and practice skills before having students work independently
are accustomed to making decisions	• involve students in setting goals and objectives • offer choices of activities • respect the students' priorities
may find planning for the future difficult	• help students to prioritize learning goals • develop supplemental activities around students' special interests • use time carefully

Adapted from *Teaching Adults: A Literacy Resource Book*, New Readers Press, 1994

▶ Working with Adult Emerging Readers

Voyager has been developed to help adult readers improve their reading and writing skills. You can employ a variety of strategies to help adult students build their skills and self-confidence. In *Voyager 2* and *Voyager 3,* students should be working to improve their word recognition strategies, fluency, and comprehension.

Improving Word Recognition

It is important that students be able to recognize words quickly, since slow word recognition disrupts both fluency and comprehension. Here are six strategies for improving word recognition.

1. **Context clues** Have students try to figure out the meaning of an unfamiliar word by using its context—the surrounding sentence and paragraph. When students come to a word they don't know, have them say "blank" and read the rest of the sentence or paragraph. Have them think of a word that would fit in the place of "blank" and reread the sentence, using the word they chose, to be sure that it makes sense.

2. **Phonics** Students need to be able to apply their phonics knowledge to help decode words.
   - When students come to a word that they can't read, ask them to underline each consonant and make the sound for each one. Then have them blend the sounds together to make a word and see if the word fits in context. *["I joined a s pp rt (support) group today."]*
   - When students have trouble with certain letter combinations (for instance, *ie*), encourage them to try the most likely pronunciation first. If the result is the correct word, the student can read on. If it is not, have the student try an alternate pronunciation.

3. **Compound Words** When students come across a word they don't know, they can check to see if it is a compound word. When students encounter a compound word they can't decode, have them draw a line between the two smaller words and read each aloud. Then have them say the two smaller words together as a compound word.

4. **Prefixes, Roots, and Suffixes** Recognizing these standard word parts can help students decode unfamiliar words.
   - Begin instruction in the analysis of word parts only when you feel individual students are ready. Continue to introduce limited numbers of new prefixes, roots, and suffixes at a measured pace. To introduce these standard word parts, refer to PCMs 8, 9, and 10.
   - Write a common prefix on a colored index card and some common roots on white index cards. (Make sure that you choose roots and prefixes that work together: *re + act, re + duce, re + flect.*) Discuss the meaning of the prefix (for example, *re-* means *back* or *again*). Have students match the prefix and roots to make new words and use the words they create in sentences. Follow the same process using roots and suffixes. Note that many common roots are not whole words.

5. **Syllabication** Several *Voyager 3* lessons teach how to divide longer words into syllables to help decode them. You can make additional lists of words to give students more practice.

6. **Sight Vocabulary** Students need to continuously build the number of words that they recognize automatically. This is especially true of the high-utility words that commonly appear in typical reading material.
   - **Flash cards** Have students make a flash card with the target word on the front. On the back, they should put either a picture representing the word or a sentence using the word. Have them make cards for 5 to 10 new words at a time. Encourage students to review the words at home. Allow time in each lesson for students to review the words. As students work with the cards, have them divide the cards into two piles—words that they recognize immediately and those they do not. Have them repeat the process until the second pile is gone.
   - **Personal dictionaries** Students can develop their own dictionaries to help them learn

sight words. Have them label each page of a notebook with a letter of the alphabet. They can write a word they want to learn and a sentence containing that word on the appropriate page. Students can also create special pages for different contexts, such as work, school, family, or other topics.

Improving Fluency

Voyager 2 and *Voyager 3* students may read hesitantly, word by word, or without expression. It is important for them to improve their fluency, because it will improve their understanding and enjoyment of written materials. Below are tips for improving reading fluency. These tips progress from low to high learner involvement.

1. **Read aloud:** Read aloud to students while they listen or follow along. In this way, you model reading with good phrasing and expression.
2. **Echo reading:** Read a sentence aloud and then have students read the same sentence aloud. Gradually increase the amount of text you read.
3. **Paired reading:** You and the students read aloud simultaneously, but you set the pace. As students' fluency increases, lower your voice so students can clearly hear their own voices.
4. **Alternate reading:** Depending on the level of the material and the ability of the student, read the first sentence or paragraph aloud. Then have the student read the next sentence or paragraph. Alternate until you have finished the selection. Students can also work in pairs, but don't pair students who both have difficulty reading fluently.

Improving Comprehension

Even if students can read all the words in a selection, they may not understand the meaning of the passage. Experience and research have shown that students get more out of reading if they use strategies that engage them actively in the reading process. The four strategies below help students improve their comprehension of reading selections.

1. **Set a purpose** Introduce a reading selection by discussing the title, any pictures or graphics, and the general topic. Discuss what students already know about the topic and what they would like to find out—their purpose for reading. (*"Find out what happens when Marla gets sick."*) When students finish the reading, ask them to discuss whether they fulfilled this purpose.
2. **Prediction** When people watch a movie or a TV show, they speculate on what is going to happen. Help students to apply this to their reading by using the following process:
    *   Before reading, discuss the title and any pictures. Have students predict what the selection will be about.
    *   While reading, stop periodically and ask questions such as, *"What do you think will happen next?"* or *"How do you think this will turn out?"* Have students check their predictions as they read. Model this by reading aloud, asking questions, and thinking through your answers aloud.
3. **Retelling** Choose two reading selections that students can read independently. Model retelling with a student as your partner. Each of you will read one of the selections silently. When you finish, tell each other about what you read. Exchange readings and repeat. Have students work in pairs to do this activity.
4. **Independent reading** In addition to working through *Voyager,* adult students should be exposed to a wide variety of other written materials. Many public libraries have special sections for adults with limited reading skills. You can also acquire high-interest, low-reading-level books—both fiction and informational reading—from New Readers Press.

Students may also need to work on their comprehension at a more specific level. The strategies below address these aspects of comprehension.

1. **Vocabulary development** Try these tips when students encounter a word they don't know the meaning of:
    *   Have students use context clues to figure out the meaning.
    *   Encourage students to add these words to their personal dictionaries.
    *   When appropriate, discuss relationships between the unfamiliar word and words they

do know. For instance, you can discuss synonyms and antonyms.

- You can also discuss classification when that is appropriate. For example, in *Voyager 2*, Lesson 5, the word *trousers* appears. You could ask students for a synonym for *trousers*. You could also ask what category *trousers* belongs to and have them name other articles of men's clothing.
- Discuss prefixes, roots, and suffixes when an unknown word contains those parts.

2. **Phrase reading** Some students read word by word rather than in phrases. They may comprehend little of what they read. To help students read in a connected and meaningful way, underline meaningful phrases or draw slashes between them. *("Marla lay in bed / with a burning pain / in her stomach.")* Then use either echo or paired reading as practice.

3. **Sentence comprehension** Some students may not be used to seeing or hearing sentences of any great complexity. As a result, they may have difficulty understanding such sentences.

Here are two suggestions for helping students:

- Have students express the sentences in their own words.
- Look at the Writing Skills Mini-Lessons on pages 60 and 86 in *Voyager 3*. Develop additional exercises in which students combine two ideas using a connecting word.

4. **Cloze exercises** This type of exercise gives students practice using nearby context clues to construct meaning. Select or create a passage that is at or below the student's reading level. Leave the first and last sentences intact and take words out of the remaining sentences. Be sure to select words for which there is some context. ("Marla lay in bed with a burning _____ in her stomach," *rather than* "_____ lay in bed with a burning pain in her _____.") You can also fill in the first letter of the deleted word. ("Marla lay in bed with a burning p_____ in her stomach.") Ask students to fill in the missing words and reread the passage to be sure each word makes sense.

▶ Working with Adult Emerging Writers

Accomplished writers have gained control over the mechanics of writing—handwriting, spelling, capitalization, punctuation, usage, and sentence structure—and can devote their attention to the composing aspects. Adult emerging writers have more difficulty because they are still struggling with both aspects of writing. These suggestions can help students with both aspects. Also included is advice about writing portfolios. As you help students improve their writing, you should

- let students write often and in uninterrupted time periods
- allow more time for writing than for skill practice
- carry out each writing assignment yourself and share your writing with students

The Writing Process

One of the keys to unlocking the talents of adult emerging writers is to work with them through the

stages of the writing process. Accomplished writers don't simply get an idea, write it down, and produce a finished piece. But inexperienced writers don't know that. They need to be taught that good writing usually involves a process that includes these five stages:

1. **Prewrite:** decide what to write about, generate ideas, and organize them
2. **Draft:** get ideas down on paper in sentence, and perhaps paragraph, form
3. **Revise:** clarify, refine, and expand the content
4. **Edit:** correct errors in grammar and mechanics
5. **Recopy:** write a final draft and share it with others

These five stages are outlined in the Reference Handbook of each student book. Here are suggestions for implementing the first four stages.

1. **Prewriting** Try these ideas to help students find topics, generate ideas, and organize their ideas:

- Have students choose topics about which they have something to say. Topics can be something that has happened to them, hobbies or interests, current events, etc. Refer to PCM 11 for other topic ideas.
- Write a word or a topic on the board and have students brainstorm ideas about it. Write all ideas down; don't dismiss anything. Review the ideas and have students select those ideas they want to use in their writing.
- Encourage students to organize their thoughts using simple outlines, lists, or graphic organizers such as those found on PCMs 3, 4, 5, and 6.

2. **Drafting** Tell students not to be concerned with spelling or grammar at this stage. Encourage them to get their ideas down on paper as they come to mind and to ask for help if they need it.

3. **Revising** Model how to revise their writing by asking questions that students should learn to ask themselves. Have a volunteer read his or her draft out loud, or read one of your own. Then ask such questions as *"Have you made the point you wanted to make? Are the ideas in an order that makes sense? Are there reasons or examples you could add to help make your point? Are there ideas that don't belong and should be taken out? Have you used the best words?"* As students become more comfortable with the process, they can work in pairs to revise their drafts. You can also prepare checklists of what to look for when revising.

4. **Editing** When students have revised their drafts to their satisfaction, help them review their work for errors in spelling, punctuation, capitalization, usage, and sentence structure. Refer students to the Writing Skills section of the Reference Handbook in their books. Help them clarify relationships between ideas by using transitions and signal words. Do not try to correct everything at once. Focus on one or two errors that occur frequently in a student's writing. Look for teachable moments when a specific skill can be practiced and reinforced.

Writing Assignments

Encourage your students to write about topics that interest them. Here are some suggestions that will help students with the composing aspects of writing.

1. **Language Experience Approach (LEA)** This approach can help students who have difficulty writing on their own. Here is one way to conduct a language experience activity.
   - Have the student tell you about a recent or important experience.
   - Write down what the student says. Ask the student to suggest a title.
   - Read the story back to the student and ask for additions or corrections.
   - Read each sentence to the student. Have the student read each sentence after you.
   - Have the student read the story aloud.
   - Have the student copy the story and put it in his or her working folder.

   Note: When working with a group, have each student contribute one sentence as you write the story on the board. Have students read the story aloud. All students then copy the story for their working folders.

2. **Journals** Encourage students to keep a journal in a notebook. Explain that they don't have to revise and edit a journal.
   - A **personal journal** includes a student's thoughts, observations, and activities. Students can keep personal journals private, or they may choose to share them.
   - A **dialogue** or **response journal** is a written dialogue between you and the student. The student writes an entry and you respond to the student's ideas and share your own. You can model corrections in your responses, but do not correct the student's writing.

The Mechanics of Writing

Here are suggestions to help students gain control over the mechanics of writing.

1. **Dictation** Writing from dictation allows students to concentrate on mechanics. Read aloud a short article or a passage from a *Voyager*

lesson. Make sure your voice indicates the appropriate punctuation—a pause for a comma, a full stop for a period, and so forth. Read slowly enough for students to keep up with you, but not so slowly that meaning is lost. When the dictation is finished, have students compare what they wrote with the printed version.

2. **Handwriting** Handwriting development can be arduous and time-intensive. Here are some ideas to keep in mind:
   - Students can practice copying words or short sentences that are meaningful to them.
   - If students print well and want to write in cursive, use PCMs 1 and 2A and B to introduce and provide handwriting practice.
   - Don't overdo handwriting practice.

3. **Spelling** Students need to understand that they need not correct every spelling error on every piece. Take a long-term approach to spelling by following these tips:
   - Have students keep a personal spelling list. They can label each page of a notebook with a letter of the alphabet. They should write words they want to know how to spell on the appropriate pages. They might also include a sentence for each target word.
   - Base spelling assignments on words that students want or need to know.
   - To keep students from getting bogged down when writing first drafts, encourage them to use invented spelling—guessing how to spell a word by the way it sounds. They can correct their spelling when they edit their drafts.
   - Make lists of words that students commonly use and misspell. Look for patterns in their errors, and teach the rules that relate to the most common mistakes.

4. **Capitalization** The Writing Skills Mini-Lesson on page 62 of *Voyager 2* introduces capitalization. The rules are repeated in the Reference Handbook. Review the rules as necessary.

5. **Sentence Structure** Several Writing Skills Mini-Lessons deal with sentence structure.
   In *Voyager 2*
   - Writing Sentences (p. 88)
   - Compound Sentences (p. 114)

   In *Voyager 3*
   - Compound Sentences (p. 34)
   - Complex Sentences (pp. 60 and 86)
   - Fixing Sentence Fragments (p. 112)

All of these mini-lessons are condensed in the Writing Skills section of the Reference Handbooks of *Voyager 2* and *Voyager 3*.

You can reinforce students' awareness and control of sentence structure by having them do the following activities. Both can be based on the reading selection in your current lesson.
- **Scrambled Sentences** Scramble the words of a sentence and write them on the board. Have students unscramble the words to write a meaningful sentence. Do this with several sentences. Students can also do this activity in pairs.
- **Key Words** Select five or six key words from an article or paragraph and write them on the board. Have students work in pairs to create a complete sentence using all the words. For practice writing compound or complex sentences, include appropriate connecting words.

Writing Portfolios

An important factor in developing confidence in writing is seeing progress over time. Have students keep all their writing in a working folder. Make sure they date each piece. Review the folders together periodically and discuss areas of improvement. Students can select special pieces to place in a writing portfolio or in a more comprehensive Personal Progress Portfolio (see p. 7). Here are some tips for developing portfolios of either type:
- Have students date and keep unfinished pieces in their working folders.
- If a student takes a piece of work through the writing process, staple the drafts together with the final product on the top. Date all pieces.
- Have students use PCM 14: Tips for Preparing a Progress Portfolio to select pieces from their working folders to include in their portfolio. Have them explain why they chose those pieces.
- Use PCM 15: Portfolio Conference Questionnaire to help students evaluate their progress.

Voyager 2 Teacher's Notes

Pre-Assessment

Before you begin Unit 1 with students, have them complete the Student Interest Inventory and the Skills Preview at the beginning of *Voyager 2* (see "Using the Student Interest Inventory" and "Using the Skills Preview," pp. 13–14).

In addition to *Voyager 2,* students will need
- folders in which to keep their finished work and

their work-in-progress (see "Working Folders," p. 7)
- a spiral-bound or three-ring notebook to use as a personal dictionary (see "Personal Dictionaries," pp. 16–17)
- a spiral-bound or three-ring notebook to use as a personal spelling list (see p. 20)

▶ Unit 1: Family Ties

Part of Unit	Voyager 2 pages	TRG pages	Workbook pages
Overview	13	21 – 22	
Lesson 1	14 – 21	22 – 23	4 – 5
Lesson 2	22 – 29	23 – 24	6 – 7
Lesson 3	30 – 35	24 – 25	8
Writing Skills Mini-Lesson	36	25	9 – 10
Unit 1 Review	37 – 38	26	11 – 13

Student Objectives

Reading
- Read a story, a letter, and a poem.
- Practice the strategies of imagining, retelling, and using prior experience.
- Understand plot, understand main idea and details, and identify rhythm and rhyme.

Writing
- Write a sequence of events, a letter, and a poem.

Speaking and Listening
- Retell, discuss, and read aloud.

Word Attack and Mechanics
- Decode words with the letter combinations *ie* and *ei, ow* and *ou.*
- Add endings that start with a vowel.

▶ Unit 1 PCMs
PCM 1: Cursive Handwriting
PCM 2: Cursive Handwriting Practice
PCM 3: Plot Map
PCM 4: Main Idea and Details Organizer

PCM 11: Writing Starters
PCM 13: Student Progress Tracking Sheet

▶ **Cursive Writing PCMs** When students are ready to learn cursive writing, introduce it using PCM 1. Suggest that they work on four or five letters per lesson, first tracing over the guidelines on the PCM, then writing each letter on a copy of PCM 2B at least 10 times. After they have practiced all the letters, they can use PCM 2A and B for practicing their signatures, writing sentences, and anything else they choose. Write practice sentences on the board as models for them.

▶ **Personal Dictionaries and Spelling Lists** Encourage students to add words they want to learn to their dictionaries and spelling lists during each lesson in Unit 1 (see above).

Unit 1 Overview (p. 13)

The overview introduces the theme "Family Ties." Discuss the collage of pictures. Tell students that they will be reading about each of the people represented in the collage. Say, *"Think about family ties. What can you guess about the family ties of these people?"* Record students' responses on the board. Read the overview aloud. Then do a paired reading with students (see "Working with Adult Emerging Readers," pp. 16–18). Discuss students' responses to the questions in the last paragraph.

Be an Active Reader Explain that as they read, "active" readers think about the information they are reading, and they try to figure out words or ideas they don't understand. Encourage students to mark things they don't understand with a question mark and to underline unknown words. After they have finished an entire selection, they can reread the marked sections to see if they now make sense.

Lesson 1 (pp. 14–21)

Learning Goals Read the learning goals aloud. Explain that Lesson 1 will focus on these goals.

Before You Read Read and discuss the first paragraph.

A–B. Read parts A and B with students. Discuss their answers.

Key Words The underlined words are important to the meaning of the reading. Have students read the sentences and try to figure out the meaning of each key word using context clues. Write the key words on the board. Ask students to read them aloud and to write words they want to learn in their personal dictionaries.

Use the Strategy Read the text aloud and discuss it. Encourage students to use the strategy of imagining to help them understand the reading. Explain that imagining helps us experience the reading more fully and understand it more clearly. Model the strategy by reading the first few lines of the selection and saying what goes through your mind as you imagine what you read. The check-ins within the reading selection remind students to apply the strategy as they read.

"Family Is Family" Before reading, discuss the picture. Follow one of the strategies outlined in

"Working with the Reading Selections" on page 14. Encourage students to mark the text as explained in "Be an Active Reader" on page 13 of *Voyager 2.* Be sure students use the check-ins to help them apply the strategy of imagining. If necessary, explain the use of quotation marks for dialogue.

After You Read

A–B. Have students reread the sections they marked and look back at words they underlined. Discuss any words or sections that they still don't understand. Remind them to add words they want to learn to their personal dictionaries.

C. Have students work as independently as possible. Encourage them to look back at the reading to confirm their answers when necessary. Discuss their responses.

Talk About It Students should understand that Ann's statement means that family members stick together no matter what. You may also want to have students discuss similar sayings, such as "Blood is thicker than water." Encourage students to write their responses.

Extending the reading: In small groups, have students discuss possible scenarios of what might happen next to Marla and her family. Say, *"Imagine the sequel to this story. What will happen with Marla, Keith, and Ann in the next week? Over the next few months?"* Write students' ideas on the board.

Think About It: Understand Plot Introduce the concept of plot in an everyday context, using a popular movie or TV show as an example. Explain that the plot is the action in a story. The plot has a beginning, a middle, and an end.

Have students read the definition of plot and its three components. Discuss the plot map. Discuss why the rising action line is so much longer than the falling action (most plots end quickly after the climax). Discuss the questions and the three parts of the plot in "Family Is Family."

Practice Students should be able to fill in the plot map by answering the three questions in their own words. For instance, the rising action might be stated, "Marla is sick and worried."

▶ *Retell* Explain that retelling means telling the events in your own words, in the order in which they occurred. Let students retell "Family Is Family" as a group. Ask volunteers to each give one event or detail of the story. One way to start retelling the story would be "'Family Is Family' is about . . ."

Talk About It Students should understand that Keith is part of the reason Marla is so worried, and that he is also the one who brings Ann back into Marla's life.

Extending the skill: Use PCM 3. Ask students to recall a story they have read or seen, or to find a story in a book or a magazine. Have them complete a plot map for the story and share their work with the class. Have students date their plot map and put it in their working folders.

Write About It: Write a Sequence of Events Read the first paragraph. Explain that the events in a story are usually written in time order—what happens first, second, and so on.

A. Have students number the events in "Family Is Family" in the order in which they happened.

B. Explain that sequence words such as *first, next,* and *then* help readers follow the order of events. Have students copy the events in the correct sequence. Then have them read the finished sentences aloud, paying special attention to the sequence words (see "Working with Adult Emerging Writers," pp. 18–20).

Writing extension: Use PCM 11, activity 5. Ask students to think of a personal experience that has special meaning for them and to write the events in sequence. Have students date their writing and put it in their working folders.

Word Work: The Vowel Combinations *ie* and *ei*
Read the introduction.

A. Point out that the *ie* combination can be pronounced as long *e* (*brief*) or as long *i* (*pie*). If necessary, remind students that a long vowel sounds like the name of the vowel.

Read aloud the *ie* words with the long *e* sound. Ask students to listen for the long *e* in each word and to repeat the word aloud. Then have students read each word aloud. Repeat this procedure for the long *i* sound. Read the tips following the lists.

B. Point out that the *ei* combination can be pronounced as long *a* (*neighbor*) or as long *e* (*ceiling*). If necessary, remind students that the *gh* is silent in words with *eigh*. Repeat the process above for the *ei* combinations. Read the tip that follows the lists. Be sure students know the meanings of all the words.

C. Read the direction line and do the first exercise with students. Encourage them to use the tips they learned to pronounce the words.

Remind students that when they are reading, they will also have the meaning of the sentence to help them figure out unknown words.

More Practice: *Voyager 2 Workbook* p. 4. The workbook exercises are designed to be done independently and should not require teacher input.

Have students fill out copies of PCM 13 to include in their working folders.

Lesson 2 (pp. 22–29)

Learning Goals Read the learning goals aloud. Explain that Lesson 2 will focus on these goals.

Before You Read Read the first paragraph with students before they do the checklist. Discuss their choices.

Next read the second paragraph, allowing students to respond to the questions. Discuss how we use shorter, easier words when we explain something to a child.

Key Words See Lesson 1 notes.

Use the Strategy Read the text and discuss it. Encourage students to use the strategy of retelling to better understand what they read. Explain that when we retell events or information in our own words, we check our comprehension of what we read. Model the strategy by reading the first few lines of the selection and asking aloud, *"What is the writer telling me about?"* Then say what goes through your mind to check your comprehension.

"To My Son" Before reading, discuss the picture. Follow one of the strategies outlined in "Working with the Reading Selections" on page 14. Be sure students use the check-ins to help apply the strategy of retelling.

After You Read See Lesson 1 notes.

Talk About It Encourage students to discuss both the benefits and drawbacks of such a discussion between father and child. Ask them to imagine what the child's point of view might be.

Extending the reading: Have students work in pairs and discuss the hopes the father has for his son. List these on the board. Then have students list hopes they have for their children or other family members.

Think About It: Understand the Main Idea and Details Read the definitions and have volunteers read the explanations. Discuss the examples from "To My Son." Discuss how the graphic organizer is shaped—so that the main idea spans all the details and the details are supports holding up the main idea. Be sure students understand the difference between the main idea and its supporting details.

Practice Read the directions. Have students complete the activity as independently as possible. Then have them compare their work in pairs.

Extending the skill: Use PCM 4. Find a short article with a clear main idea and details. (You can find such an article in *News for You*, the newspaper published by New Readers Press.) Have students read the article and complete the organizer.

Write About It: Write a Letter Read and discuss the first paragraph.
A. Help students complete this list if necessary. Encourage them to think of a child they know as they prewrite.
B. Discuss the format of letters: the salutation, the body, the closing, and the signature. Look back at "To My Son" as an example. Then let

students use the letter starter provided to write their letters as independently as possible (see "Working with Adult Emerging Writers," pp. 18–20).

Word Work: The Letter Combinations *ow* and *ou*
A–C. See Lesson 1 notes. Stress the strategy of trying the most common sounds first: long *o* for *ow* and *ou* as in *out*. If needed, point out that the letters *gh* can either be silent (*dough* and *bought*) or have the sound *f* (*rough*). Explain that *couldn't* is a contraction formed from *could* and *not*. Ask what words *wouldn't* and *shouldn't* are formed from.

More Practice: *Voyager 2 Workbook* p. 6

Have students fill out copies of PCM 13 to include in their working folders.

Lesson 3 (pp. 30–35)

Learning Goals Read the learning goals aloud. Explain that Lesson 3 will focus on these goals.

Before You Read Read the introduction.
A. Read the questions and discuss students' answers.
B. Discuss students' responses to the checklist. Explain that poetry is a special type of writing in which the poet chooses specific words to convey images (mental pictures) and emotions, and that poets often use conventions, such as rhyme and rhythm. Discuss how poems look— they often have one phrase per line, and they're often short. Explain that each word is carefully chosen. Have students name or recite poems they know. Tell them that limericks, song lyrics, and nursery rhymes are types of poems.

Key Words See Lesson 1 notes.

Use the Strategy Explain to students that their experiences are a rich resource they can tap into as they read. Tell them they will use their experiences to better understand the poem in this lesson. By comparing situations in a reading to their own experiences, students can personally relate to what they are reading and predict possible outcomes.

"The Quarrel" Before reading, discuss the picture. Read the poem aloud; then do a paired reading with students. Finally, let students read the poem aloud on their own. Be sure they apply the strategy of using prior experience by comparing events in the poem with events in their own lives.

After You Read See Lesson 1 notes.

Talk About It Extend the discussion by asking, *"Why do we often feel we are right and the other person is wrong? Why is it sometimes so hard to see the other person's point of view?"*

Extending the reading: Have students compare and contrast the content of "The Quarrel" and "Family Is Family," the story from Lesson 1. Explain that when we compare, we notice similarities; when we contrast, we notice differences. Ask, *"Who was quarreling in each reading? Who made the first move to make up? How did the arguments end?"* List answers on the board under the headings "Similarities" and "Differences." Then ask students which reading they preferred and why.

Think About It: Identify Rhythm and Rhyme

Rhythm Ask students to explain rhythm. Suggest they think in terms of music. Discuss their explanations. Then read the description of rhythm aloud. Have students read the line from "The Quarrel" and clap to the rhythm.

Rhyme Read the description of rhyme. Ask students to provide more examples of rhyming words.
A–B. Work through these exercises with students. Be sure to read the last paragraph of part B aloud. Add other examples (for example, *phone* and *groan* rhyme; *head* and *bead* do not).

Practice Do the first exercise in A and B with students. Then let them complete the work alone or with a partner.

Extending the skill: Have students clap the rhythm and find the rhyming words of a well-known poem or song.

Write About It: Write a Poem Read and discuss the first paragraph.
A. As part of the prewriting activity, ask students to list things they fight over with a family

member and things that make them laugh or cry with this person. Write their ideas on the board. Read the reminder about rhyme and rhythm being optional in a poem.
B. Tell students they can complete the lines of the poem given or they can write their own poem. If they want their poem to rhyme, they should choose words for the end of each line that rhyme with many other words.

Talk About It Have students answer specific questions about their partner's poem: Was it clear? Did the lines make sense? For students who used rhyme, have their partners find the rhyming words in their poems. For those who used a regular rhythm, have their partners clap out the rhythm of their poems.

More Practice: *Voyager 2 Workbook* p. 8

Have students fill out copies of PCM 13 to include in their working folders.

Writing Skills Mini-Lesson: Adding Endings That Start with a Vowel (p. 36)

Read the first paragraph. Explain that endings are letters added to the ends of words. Give several common examples (*help: helping, helper, helpful*). Explain that spelling rules apply when adding endings that start with a vowel.
1. Read and discuss the first rule and examples. Point out that these words, like most words, did not change when the endings were added. Ask students for other examples.
2–4. Read and discuss the other rules and examples. Make sure that students understand one rule before you move on to the next one. Ask students for other examples for each rule.

Practice When students seem comfortable with the rules, have them do the paragraph exercise. You can have students work in pairs. Have students date their writing and put it in their working folders.

More Practice: *Voyager 2 Workbook* p. 9

Unit 1 Review (pp. 37–38)

Explain that this review will help students evaluate what they have learned in Unit 1.

Reading Review Have students complete the questions as independently as possible.

Writing Process Before students begin the Writing Process, have them turn to page 128 in their books. Discuss the five steps of the writing process. Explain that students have already completed steps 1 and 2 for the three pieces they wrote in Unit 1. Help students locate the draft they want to work with further. Work with students as they revise, edit, and create a final draft.

To help students with the revising step, go over the specific point listed for each type of draft. When they get to the editing step, remind students to check the spelling of words that have endings. Have students date their final drafts and put them in their working folders.

Extending the theme: To extend the theme of "Family Ties" in Unit 1, suggest that students make family trees showing their parents, grandparents, and, if relevant, children and grandchildren. Ask if any students or their family members have researched their family tree.

More Practice: *Voyager 2 Workbook* p. 11

▶ *Final Note:* Review with students the copies of PCM 13 that they placed in their working folders. Ask what additional help they think they need with material from the three lessons and the Writing Skills Mini-Lesson in Unit 1. Discuss possible ways of meeting those needs.

▶ Unit 2: Life Goes On

Part of Unit	Voyager 2 pages	TRG pages	Workbook pages
Overview	39	27	
Lesson 4	40 – 47	27 – 28	14 – 15
Lesson 5	48 – 53	29 – 30	16
Lesson 6	54 – 61	30 – 31	17 – 18
Writing Skills Mini-Lesson	62	31	19 – 20
Unit 2 Review	63 – 64	31	21 – 23

Student Objectives

Reading
- Read a story, poems, and a biography.
- Use the reading strategies of imagining, prior knowledge, and retelling.
- Understand character, understand the use of repetition, and make inferences.

Writing
- Write a note, a poem, and a letter.

Speaking and Listening
- Discuss, read aloud, and retell.

Word Attack and Mechanics
- Learn and review the use of basic context clues.
- Learn the rules for capitalization.

▶ Unit 2 PCMs
PCM 1: Cursive Handwriting
PCM 2: Cursive Handwriting Practice
PCM 5: Character Web
PCM 6: Story Frame
PCM 7: Using a Dictionary
PCM 11: Writing Starters
PCM 12: Map of the United States
PCM 13: Student Progress Tracking Sheet

▶ Cursive Writing PCMs
Use PCM 1 and 2B with students who are continuing to practice four or five letters per lesson. Use PCM 2A and B with students who need practice writing their names and sentences. Write practice words and sentences on the board as models.

▶ Personal Dictionaries and Spelling Lists
Encourage students to add words they want to learn to their dictionaries and spelling lists during each lesson in Unit 2 (see p. 21).

Unit 2 Overview (p. 39)

The overview introduces the theme "Life Goes On" with a collage of pictures from the three readings in the unit. Ask, *"What does the phrase 'life goes on' mean to you? What ideas does it bring to mind?"* Read the overview aloud, then do a paired reading. Discuss the questions in the last paragraph.

Be an Active Reader See Unit 1 notes.

Lesson 4 (pp. 40–47)

Learning Goals Discuss the learning goals.

Before You Read Read the first paragraph and discuss students' responses.
A–B. Read aloud as needed. Discuss students' answers.

Have students locate California, the setting of the story, on PCM 12. Use a globe or world map to show students where Mexico is located. (*Note:* Have students keep their copy of PCM 12 for future reference.)

Key Word See Lesson 1 notes.

Use the Strategy Tell students they will use the strategy of imagining introduced in Lesson 1. Using this strategy, they will try to see, hear, and feel what is going on between two friends. This will help them better understand the reading.

"Saying Good-bye" Before reading, discuss the picture. Follow one of the strategies outlined in "Working with the Reading Selections" on page 14. Be sure students use the check-ins as reminders to apply the strategy of imagining. Remind students that quotation marks enclose the words the two friends say to each other.

After You Read See Lesson 1 notes.

Talk About It Students should understand that even though Rosa is calm on the outside, she is scared and upset on the inside. Discuss with students how they have reacted when they heard bad news from a family member or friend. Ask, *"What did you say to the other person? How did you feel on the inside?"*

Extending the reading: Have volunteers role-play the story in pairs, each taking the part of either Rosa or Carmen. Pairs could also role-play an imaginary scene between Carmen and Hector, in which Hector and Carmen talk about his new job and Carmen wonders how she will break the news to Rosa. Allow time for students to practice their role plays.

Think About It: Understand Character Introduce the concept by using a character from a movie or TV show as an example. Have students name their favorite movie or TV character and tell what they like about the character. List students' responses and discuss them.

Have students read the definition of character and the list that follows it. Discuss the character web and the two qualities that students choose to complete Carmen's character web.

Practice Encourage students to look back at the story to make their list that describes Rosa. Have them complete the character web independently. Discuss their responses.

Extending the skill: Provide copies of a short story or an excerpt from a story that develops a character well, or use "Family Is Family" from Lesson 1. Have students read the selection and complete the character web on PCM 5. Have students date their work and put it in their working folders.

Write About It: Write a Note Read the first paragraph.

A. Explain that writers often use a list to gather their thoughts and ideas before writing. Ask students to list a few things they could suggest to Rosa to help her cope after Carmen moves away.

B. Tell students to use their lists to complete a note to Rosa. They should fill in the date, write their ideas in sentences, and sign the note.

Writing extension: Have students use PCM 6 to develop a story frame for "Saying Good-bye." Students should refer to the story to find out where it takes place, the rising action, the climax or turning point, and the falling action. Have students date their work and put it in their working folders.

Word Work: Context Clues Read the introduction. Point out that when experienced readers don't know a word in a sentence, they read the rest of the sentence or paragraph and try to figure out what the word means. They are using context clues to help them decode unknown words.

Read the first paragraph and the example aloud. Ask students to guess what word completes the sentence. Tell them to ask themselves, "What word makes sense here?" Then read the next two paragraphs, which explain how to determine that the missing word is *interview.*

Practice Read the directions and help students with the exercise. Encourage students to ask, "What word makes sense here?" for each sentence.

Word Work extension: If you feel students are ready to start using a dictionary, give them PCM 7. Explain that it is a good idea to check the definition of an unknown word in a dictionary. If necessary, review and practice alphabetical order. Do one or more of the activities designed to familiarize students with dictionaries. Demonstrate how to use guide words, and have students practice this skill. Encourage students to develop the habit of looking up unknown words.

More Practice: *Voyager 2 Workbook* p. 14

Have students fill out copies of PCM 13 to include in their working folders.

Lesson 5 (pp. 48–53)

Learning Goals Discuss the learning goals.

Before You Read Read the first two paragraphs. Discuss different causes of grief and why people grieve. Volunteers may share personal experiences of loss and grief.

Have students complete the checklist. Discuss their responses. Ask for other words or phrases that describe how grieving people feel.

Key Words See Lesson 1 notes.

Use the Strategy Point out that students will use their personal knowledge to better understand the poetry in this lesson. Explain that when we use this strategy, we recall what we know about a topic to more fully understand what we are reading.

"Lament" Discuss the picture. Read the poem aloud; then do a paired reading with students. Remind students to use their prior knowledge as they read the poem. Remind them also to keep on reading if there is no end mark at the end of a line. Explain that reading in this way will help them better understand the poem.

After You Read See Lesson 1 notes.

Talk About It Make sure students consider the fact that when people suffer a great loss, they often can focus only on one day at a time. They use all their strength to hold themselves or their family together and make it through the day. Extend the discussion by asking: *"Do you think the woman really means that the 'dead [should] be forgotten'?"*

Extending the reading: Ask students to work in pairs using PCM 5 to do a character web of the woman in the poem. To help them, ask: *"Is this woman married, single, divorced, or widowed? How many children does she have? What things will she do to help her cope with the loss of her husband? What qualities does she have, based on what we read in the poem?"* Have students write the word *woman* in the center oval and complete the web with information about the woman.

Think About It: Understand the Use of Repetition Discuss how repetition is used to emphasize certain ideas.

Read the introductory paragraph aloud. Then read "Lament" aloud and have students listen for the repeated line.

Read the poem again, asking students to pay attention to the three lines that follow the repeated lines. Then read and discuss the paragraphs that interpret these lines.

Practice Read and discuss the introduction to the poem. Ask students what they know about the Nazi concentration camps in World War II. Have them imagine how hard life was for people who were sent to concentration camps. Have volunteers read the poem aloud. Then have students answer the questions independently. Discuss their answers.

Extending the skill: Find a poem that makes strong use of repetition to get its meaning across. Or ask students to suggest a favorite poem, song, or other writing that uses repetition. Have them identify the repetition and analyze its effect.

Write About It: Write a Poem Read and discuss the first paragraph.
A. Encourage students to picture what they would like to change and how they would like to be from today on.
B. Discuss the structure of the poem. Have students read the poem starters before filling in the blanks so that they can get a sense of what to do. Tell them to reread "From Tomorrow On." Explain that their poems will use the same structure, but should focus on what they would like to change "from today on."

Talk About It Write the headings "Similarities" and "Differences" on the board. Ask students to compare and contrast the ways of coping of the speakers in the two poems—the adult and the child. Ask, *"Do you think children's innocence helps them cope better with loss?"*

More Practice: *Voyager 2 Workbook* p. 16

Have students fill out copies of PCM 13 to include in their working folders.

Lesson 6 (pp. 54–61)

Learning Goals Discuss the learning goals.

Before You Read Read and discuss the introduction. Explain that a biography is a true account of the important events in a real person's life. Be sure students understand that a biography is not about a fictional character.

A–B. Read aloud as needed. Discuss students' answers.

Key Words See Lesson 1 notes.

Use the Strategy Tell students they will use the strategy of retelling introduced in Lesson 2 to better understand the reading. Remind them that we retell what we have read by putting it into our own words. By asking, *"What is the writer telling me now?"* we check our comprehension as we read.

"Life in the Hearing World" Discuss the picture. Follow one of the strategies outlined in "Working with the Reading Selections" on page 14. Explain that this biography tells events in sequence. Remind students to use the check-ins to help them apply the strategy of retelling.

After You Read See Lesson 1 notes.

Talk About It After students retell Michael's story to a partner or small group, start a discussion by asking, *"If you were deaf, how would you communicate with hearing people? Take classes? Look for a job? Find an apartment?"*

Extending the reading: To help students understand how a deaf person deals with life in a hearing world, ask them to communicate with a partner without speaking. For instance, they might act out buying a shirt or going out to eat. If students are interested, invite someone who knows American Sign Language to visit the class. Discuss how learning to sign is similar to and different from learning to read.

Think About It: Make Inferences Explain that writers don't always state their ideas directly. Sometimes readers have to "read between the lines" to understand ideas.

Read the introduction and work through the examples with students. If necessary, model inferring with another example from the reading: *"'When Michael was in his twenties, Prince died. He decided he did not need another hearing-ear dog.' Because Michael felt he no longer needed to rely on a dog, I can infer that Michael felt he could make it on his own."*

Practice Have students read the excerpts and answer the questions alone or with a partner. Discuss students' answers.

Extending the skill: Have students compile a list of everything they know about Michael Delani. Then they should note whether they were told (**T**) or inferred (**I**) each piece of information.

Write About It: Write a Letter Read and discuss the introduction.

A. Explain that when getting ready to write, we often think of as many ideas as possible and then select the best ones. Before students begin their lists, ask volunteers to brainstorm questions they might ask Michael. Write the ideas on the board.

B. Review the format of a letter. Have students write the date, complete the body of the letter with their own questions for Michael, and sign the letter. Have students share their letters with a partner or small group.

Word Work: Context Clues Read the introduction and discuss the example with students. Ask which words helped them figure out the correct meaning of the phrase.

Read the directions. Have students complete the exercise independently and discuss their answers.

Word Work extension: Continue to use PCM 7 to help students become familiar with using a dictionary.

More Practice: *Voyager 2 Workbook* p. 17

Have students fill out copies of PCM 13 to include in their working folders.

Writing Skills Mini-Lesson: Using Capital Letters (p. 62)

Read the introduction.

1. Read the first rule and examples. Point out that capitalizing the first word of a sentence helps us know when a new sentence begins.
2. Read the second rule and examples. Ask students to give other examples of days of the week, holidays, and months. Write the words on the board for students to copy.
3. Read the third rule and examples. Have students write their own city, state, and country. Point out that words such as *library* and *school* also name places, but they are capitalized only when they appear in the name of a specific library or school (for example, *Lincoln Library, Mahalia Jackson School*).
4. Read the fourth rule and examples. Have students write their own names and appropriate titles.

Practice When students feel comfortable with these rules, have them do the paragraph exercise on a separate piece of paper. Have students date their writing and put it in their working folders.

More Practice: *Voyager 2 Workbook* p. 19

Unit 2 Review (pp. 63–64)

Follow the process described in Unit 1. As students edit their writing, have them check that they added endings and capitalized words correctly. Have students date their writing and put it in their working folders.

Extending the theme: To extend the theme of "Life Goes On," use PCM 11. Ask students to do the third activity in number 4. Have them choose a character from one of the readings in Unit 2 to write about. Ask how they would have made sure that "life goes on." Have students date their writing and put it in their working folders.

More Practice: *Voyager 2 Workbook* p. 21

▶ *Final Note:* Review with students the copies of PCM 13 that they have placed in their working folders. Ask what additional help they think they need with the material from the three lessons and the Writing Skills Mini-Lesson in Unit 2. Discuss possible ways of meeting those needs.

▶ Unit 3: New Beginnings

Part of Unit	Voyager 2 pages	TRG pages	Workbook pages
Overview	65	32	
Lesson 7	66 – 71	32 – 33	24
Lesson 8	72 – 79	33 – 34	25 – 26
Lesson 9	80 – 87	34 – 36	27 – 28
Writing Skills Mini-Lesson	88	36	29 – 30
Unit 3 Review	89 – 90	36	31 – 33

Student Objectives

Reading
- Read a song, a journal, and a student's autobiography.
- Practice the strategies of using prior knowledge, imagining, and retelling.
- Make inferences and understand the main idea and details.

Writing
- Write a reaction to a song, a journal entry, and interview questions and results.

Speaking and Listening
- Read aloud, discuss, and interview.

Word Attack and Mechanics
- Decode and identify compound words.
- Understand prefixes and roots.
- Write correct sentences.

▶ Unit 3 PCMs
PCM 4: Main Idea and Details Organizer
PCM 8: Common Prefixes
PCM 9: Common Roots
PCM 11: Writing Starters
PCM 12: Map of the United States
PCM 13: Student Progress Tracking Sheet

▶ Personal Dictionaries and Spelling Lists
Encourage students to add words they want to learn to their dictionaries and spelling lists during each lesson in Unit 3 (see p. 21).

Unit 3 Overview (p. 65)

The overview introduces the theme "New Beginnings." Discuss the collage of pictures. Tell students the new beginnings they will read about in the unit are represented in the collage. Say, *"Think about new beginnings. What new beginnings might the people pictured have had?"* Record students' responses on the board. Read the overview aloud. Then do a paired reading with students (see "Working with Adult Emerging Readers," pp. 16–18). Discuss students' responses to the questions in the last paragraph.

Be an Active Reader See Unit 1 notes.

Lesson 7 (pp. 66–71)

Learning Goals Discuss the learning goals.

Before You Read Read and discuss the information about the song and the code it contains. Ask students to share what they know about slavery in the U.S. List their responses on the board. Discuss the question in the last paragraph.

Key Word See Lesson 1 notes.

Use the Strategy Tell students that they will use their prior knowledge to more fully understand the song in this lesson. Remind students that when we use this strategy, we recall information we already know about a topic to better understand new information that we're reading.

"Follow the Drinking Gourd" Discuss the picture. Read the lyrics with students, following the rhythm of the chorus as marked below.[1]

```
 /  _   _   /   /   /
Fol - low // the drink - ing gourd.
```

```
 /  _   _   /   /   /
Fol - low // the drink - ing gourd.
```

```
 _  _  /  /  /  _  /  _  _  _  /  _  _  _  /  _
For the old man is a - wait - ing for to car - ry you to free - dom
```

```
 _  _  /  _  _  /  /  /
If you fol - low the drink - ing gourd.
```

Read the lyrics again, clapping or tapping the rhythm. Ask if any students are familiar with the tune of this song. If so, encourage them to teach it to the class. Remind students to use the check-ins to help them apply the strategy of using prior knowledge.

After You Read See Lesson 1 notes.

Talk About It Ask students to imagine what a new beginning would have meant to slaves. Discuss the sort of life that escaped slaves faced. Be sure students understand that most slaves could not read or write.

Extending the reading: Use PCM 12 to locate the states that allowed slavery in the mid-1800s: Alabama, Arkansas, Delaware, Florida, Georgia, Kentucky, Louisiana, Maryland, Mississippi, Missouri, North Carolina, South Carolina, Tennessee, Texas, and Virginia (which included present-day West Virginia). If possible, display a map of Underground Railroad routes from an encyclopedia and have students trace these routes on their maps.

Think About It: Make Inferences Read the introduction and work through the example with students. Discuss using prior knowledge and clues to make inferences.

Practice Have students reread the song before they answer the questions.

Extending the skill: Find a short story that you can read aloud in less than 10 minutes. Identify places where inferences can be made. Distribute copies of the story to students. Read the story aloud as students follow along. Stop at the places where inferences can be made, and have students infer information from the clues. Help them by asking such questions as *"Why do you think the person did that?"* or *"Who do you think did that?"*

Write About It: Write About a Song Read the introduction.
A. Allow students time to think about the suggested questions. Encourage them to add questions of their own. Have students write their ideas on separate paper.
B. Have students write first drafts using their prewriting ideas. They may complete the sentence starters provided and/or write their own sentences. When students have finished, invite them to share their thoughts with a partner or group.

More Practice: *Voyager 2 Workbook* p. 24

Have students fill out copies of PCM 13 to include in their working folders.

Lesson 8 (pp. 72–79)

Learning Goals Discuss the learning goals.

Before You Read Read and discuss the first two paragraphs. Explain that people write in journals for a variety of reasons. Some people keep a journal to record everyday events. Others use journals to record inner thoughts and feelings.
A–B. Read aloud as needed. Discuss students' answers.

Key Words See Lesson 1 notes.

Use the Strategy Tell students that they will use the strategy of imagining they practiced in Lessons 1 and 4. Point out that if they can imagine how a

---

1. / indicates a stressed syllable; _ indicates an unstressed syllable; // indicates a pause

man whose wife had just left him would think and feel, they will better understand the journal entries.

"Al's Journal" Discuss the picture. Follow one of the strategies outlined in "Working with the Reading Selections" on page 14. Remind students to use the check-ins to help them apply the strategy of imagining. Point out that Al's journal entries are written on different dates during a one-month period.

After You Read See Lesson 1 notes.

Talk About It Discuss students' responses. Ask students to imagine how Al's daughters must feel about the divorce and to talk about how Al might help them cope.

Extending the reading: Using PCM 11, discuss with students the meaning of each saying in activity 3. Then ask students to choose one of the sayings and write about how it applies to Al's marriage problems. Have students date their writing and put it in their working folders.

Think About It: Understand the Main Idea and Details Read the first paragraph. Discuss how important it is to understand a writer's main idea, even though it is not always stated.

Read the example of the June 6 journal entry. Have students first choose the main idea and then underline at least three details that support it. Tell them to ask themselves about each detail in the entry, *"Does this describe a marriage that is ending?"*

Practice

A. Have students do the exercise as independently as possible.

B. Point out that some statements do not give a reason that marriages fail, and so they are not *supporting* details for that main idea.

Extending the skill: Use PCM 4. Have students reread "Life in the Hearing World" in Lesson 6. Help them identify the main idea and write it in the top of the organizer. Then have students find four supporting details and write them under the main idea.

Write About It: Write a Journal Entry Read the first paragraph. Remind students that a journal is often kept private because it reveals a person's thoughts and feelings. Explain that because a journal is not usually meant for others to read, the writer does not take the time to prewrite journal entries. Instead, the writer writes down thoughts as they come to mind.

Ask students to think about the topic "A Hard Time in My Life" and jot down notes if they like. Then have students write a journal entry on the topic. Be sure they understand that they don't have to share this writing.

Encourage students to start their own journals in separate notebooks.

Word Work: Compound Words Read the first paragraph. Ask if students can find a compound word other than *bedroom* in the first paragraph *(sometimes)*. Encourage them to suggest other examples. List these on the board.

A–B. Read the directions and have students do the exercises independently.

Word Work extension: Bring in copies of a story or news article that contains compound words. Have students read the story, underline the compound words, and identify the smaller words within them.

More Practice: *Voyager 2 Workbook* p. 25

Have students fill out copies of PCM 13.

Lesson 9 (pp. 80–87)

Learning Goals Discuss the learning goals.

Before You Read Read the first paragraph. Explain that an autobiography is written by a person about his or her life. In "A New World," Mamie Chow, an adult student, tells what it was like for her to move to a new country.

A–B. List students' responses on the board and discuss them.

Key Words See Lesson 1 notes.

Use the Strategy Point out that students will again be using the strategy of retelling to better understand the reading in the lesson.

"A New World" Discuss the picture. Follow one of the strategies outlined in "Working with the Reading Selections" on page 14. Be sure students use the check-ins as reminders to apply the strategy of retelling. Review the concept of sequence with students. Tell them they will read about the events of Mamie Chow's life in the order in which they happened.

After You Read See Lesson 1 notes.

Talk About It Review the list of problems made in response to part A of "Before You Read." Ask, *"Which of these problems did Mamie Chow face? What other problems did she face? Do other newcomers to this country have different kinds of problems?"* Invite students to share "success stories" of newcomers they know.

Extending the reading: Have students work with a partner to create a list of important events in Mamie Chow's life. They should complete this list in time sequence. For instance, students might begin: 1. Mamie Chow's marriage was arranged by her parents. 2. Mamie Chow left China in 1948. Students should refer to the reading for other important events in Mamie Chow's life.

Think About It: Make Inferences Read the first two paragraphs. Have a volunteer read the excerpt from "A New World." Be sure students understand that they have to make educated guesses, based on the information given, about the kind of daughter Mamie Chow was. The passage doesn't state this directly, but there are many clues that tell how she behaved as a daughter and how she related to her parents. Let students complete the checklist alone or in pairs.

Practice Read the directions. Have students complete the practice as independently as possible. Discuss the inferences they made and ask them to explain their responses.

Extending the skill: Return to a previous story students have read, such as "Family Is Family" in Lesson 1 or "Saying Good-bye" in Lesson 4. Read the story with students, stopping at points where inferences about characters, motivation, or events might be made. Ask students what inferences they can make at these points. Also discuss when inferences may *not* be made because of lack of information. For example, in "Family Is Family," you cannot infer that Marla is divorced, only that she lives alone with her son.

Write About It: Conduct and Write an Interview Read and discuss the introduction.

A. Help students prepare their questions. A good *what* question for any new beginning is: "What did you do?" A good *why* question might be: "Why did you do it?" Have students write their questions on a separate piece of paper, leaving space between questions to take notes on the answers.

B. Help students write a good first sentence. For example, "[Partner's name] made a new beginning when he/she got a new job." Students can use their notes from the interview to finish the paragraph.

Word Work: Prefixes and Roots The activities on this page are challenging. Allow plenty of time to introduce and practice this recognition strategy.

Read and discuss the three explanatory paragraphs with students. Explain that recognizing prefixes and roots can help them identify unfamiliar words. Experienced readers see if they can break unfamiliar words into parts—roots and prefixes—to figure out their meanings.

Read the prefix chart. Be sure students understand what each column contains and how to read across the rows. Ask students for other examples of words that begin with the prefixes *un-, re-,* and *anti-*. List their responses on the board.

A–B. Read the directions and help students with the exercises. When they are finished, discuss what each word means. Ask if any of the words were unfamiliar. Remind students to add words they want to learn to their personal dictionaries.

Word Work extension: When students understand the concept of prefixes, begin using PCMs 8 and 9. Read the first few prefixes on PCM 8, their meanings, and example words. Point out that *dis-* and *in-* have more than one spelling, depending on the root that follows. When students are ready, help them select roots from PCM 9 to form another word with each prefix. Have them write this example. Point out that many roots are not whole words in English. Continue working with prefixes and roots in this manner in subsequent lessons.

More Practice: *Voyager 2 Workbook* p. 27

Have students fill out copies of PCM 13.

Writing Skills Mini-Lesson: Writing Sentences (p. 88)

1. Read the first rule and the examples. Explain that the first thought is not complete because it leaves questions unanswered. For example, it doesn't tell who is doing what to prepare for a career.
2. Read the second rule and examples. Point out that without both a subject and a verb, a sentence is not complete. Have students name the subject and verb in each sentence. Ask them to suggest other sentences. Write these on the board and help students identify the subject and verb in each.
3. Read rule 3 and the examples. Write other sentences on the board and ask students to correct capitalization and punctuation.

Practice When students feel comfortable with these rules, have them do the rewriting exercise on separate paper. Then ask volunteers to read their sentences aloud. Discuss the different ways each fragment can be made a complete sentence. You can also use PCM 11, activity 1 or 2, to reinforce writing complete sentences. Have students date their writing and put it in their working folders.

More Practice: *Voyager 2 Workbook* p. 29

Unit 3 Review (pp. 89–90)

Follow the process described in Unit 1. As students edit their writing, have them check that they added endings, capitalized words, and wrote complete sentences correctly. Have students date their writing and put it in their working folders.

Extending the theme: Use PCM 11, activity 6. Have students think about an important decision they have made and write about it, answering the questions on the PCM. Have students date their writing and put it in their working folders.

More Practice: *Voyager 2 Workbook* p. 31

▶ *Final Note:* Review with students the copies of PCM 13 that they have placed in their working folders. Ask what additional help they think they need with the material from the three lessons and the Writing Skills Mini-Lesson in Unit 3. Discuss possible ways of meeting those needs.

▶ Unit 4: Celebrate Differences

Part of Unit	Voyager 2 pages	TRG pages	Workbook pages
Overview	91	37	
Lesson 10	92 – 99	37 – 38	34 – 35
Lesson 11	100 – 107	38 – 39	36 – 37
Lesson 12	108 – 113	39 – 40	38
Writing Skills Mini-Lesson	114	40 – 41	39 – 40
Unit 4 Review	115 – 116	41	41 – 43

Student Objectives

Reading

- Read a story, a biography, a poem, and a song.
- Practice the strategies of using prior experience and prior knowledge.
- Understand plot and character; make inferences; and identify rhyme, rhythm, and repetition.

Writing

- Write a description, an autobiography, and a poem.

Speaking and Listening

- Retell, discuss, and read aloud.

Word Attack and Mechanics

- Understand prefixes, roots, and suffixes.
- Combine simple sentences to form compound sentences.

▶ Unit 4 PCMs

PCM 3: Plot Map
PCM 5: Character Web
PCM 9: Common Roots
PCM 10: Common Suffixes
PCM 11: Writing Starters
PCM 12: Map of the United States
PCM 13: Student Progress Tracking Sheet

▶ Personal Dictionaries and Spelling Lists

Encourage students to add words they want to learn to their dictionaries and spelling lists during each lesson in Unit 4 (see p. 21).

Unit 4 Overview (p. 91)

The overview introduces the theme "Celebrate Differences." Discuss the collage of pictures. Tell students they represent the three readings in Unit 4. Have volunteers read the overview. Ask students to think about the many different cultures in the United States. Discuss the questions in the second paragraph and record students' answers on the board.

Be an Active Reader See Unit 1 notes.

Lesson 10 (pp. 92–99)

Learning Goals Discuss the learning goals.

Before You Read Read and discuss the background information about three different cultural celebrations. If necessary, help students with three words in the introduction—*kinara, karamu,* and *menorah.* List on the board the holidays students mention in response to the last paragraph.

Use the Strategy Tell students that they will use their personal experience to better understand the reading in this lesson. Explain that recalling celebrations that are part of their cultural heritage will help them get the most out of the story.

"Neighborly Celebrations" Discuss the picture. Follow one of the strategies outlined in "Working with the Reading Selections" on page 14. Be sure students use the check-ins to apply the strategy of using prior experience. As they read, they should ask themselves, "How does this celebration compare with my own?"

After You Read See Lesson 1 notes.

Talk About It Encourage students to draw on their own experiences and knowledge during the discussion. Ask, *"How were the celebrations like ones your families have? How were they different?"*

Extending the reading: Make a chart on the board listing the similarities and differences students found among the three holidays described in the story. Have students copy the chart.

Think About It: Understand Plot and Character

Read the introduction and discuss the three elements of the plot diagram—rising action (introduces the characters and the problem); climax (event that solves the problem); and falling action (events that draw the story to a close).

Read and discuss the information about character.

Practice Have students do the plot and character exercises as independently as possible. Then have them form pairs and retell the story (question 7).

Extending the skill: Find a short story that has a well-defined plot. Have students read the story and complete the plot map on PCM 3 to record the rising action, the climax, and the falling action. Have students complete a character web for Wanda Mays, using PCM 5.

Write About It: Write a Description Read the introduction.

A. Have students use the idea map to help them generate ideas about how they celebrate their favorite holiday.

B. Have students write descriptions of their favorite holiday using their idea maps. Remind them to use complete sentences.

Word Work: Suffixes *-ful, -less, -able, -or* Review the definitions of prefix and root. Read the first two paragraphs aloud. Explain the reading tip in the second paragraph. Demonstrate with *careful.*

Read the introduction to the chart and then each row of the chart. Ask students to give additional examples of words with the suffixes *-ful, -less, -able,* and *-or.* List their examples on the board.

A–B. Read the directions and have students do the exercises as independently as possible. Then have students tell the meaning of each word with the suffix added. Ask volunteers to use the words in sentences.

Word Work extension: Use PCM 10. Read the first few suffixes, their meanings, and examples.

Provide a second example for each suffix. Ask students to write another example for each suffix by matching each suffix to a root from PCM 9. If students suggest a word that requires a spelling change to the root, point this out. Continue working with suffixes and roots in this manner in subsequent lessons.

More Practice: *Voyager 2 Workbook* p. 34

Have students fill out copies of PCM 13.

Lesson 11 (pp. 100–107)

Learning Goals Discuss the learning goals.

Before You Read Read the introductory paragraph. Remind students that a biography is a true account of a person's life.

A–B. Have students complete these exercises independently and discuss their answers with a partner or small group.

Have students locate Hawaii and the Pacific Ocean on PCM 12. Then have them locate Hawaii, Japan, and the United States on a globe or world map so students can see the relative distances between them.

Key Words See Lesson 1 notes.

Use the Strategy Tell students that they will apply the strategy of using their knowledge to better understand the reading in this lesson. Ask students to recall what they know about biographies. Then, as they read, they should look for the kind of information they expect to find.

"Celebrate an American Life" Discuss the picture. Follow one of the strategies outlined in "Working with the Reading Selections" on page 14. Be sure students use the check-ins to apply the strategy of using prior knowledge. Point out that the biography is written in time sequence. It begins with Daniel Inouye's birthday and progresses through the stages of his life.

After You Read See Lesson 1 notes.

Talk About It To extend the discussion, ask, *"Have you or someone you know ever been discriminated against because of race, culture, religion, sex, or* *other reason? What happened? How did you feel about it?"*

Extending the reading

1. Use PCM 11. Have students complete activity 2, writing about "Celebrate an American Life." They should refer to the reading to write their sentences. Have students date their writing and put it in their working folders.

2. Using PCM 5, ask students to complete a character web of a famous person from a different ethnic or cultural background. It may be an entertainer, an educator, a politician, an athlete, or someone in another field. If students need help getting started, ask *"Is the person male or female? Is the person alive today? What is the person famous for? What is the person's race? What has the person accomplished? What do you admire about this person?"*

Think About It: Make Inferences Discuss with students how readers need to fill in missing details by making inferences.

Read the first paragraph. Allow time for students to read the cartoon. Ask what they can infer about different cultural groups by reading the cartoon. Discuss their responses to the question near the bottom of the page. Read the paragraph that follows it aloud. Ask if students agree.

Practice Have students do the exercise independently. Discuss their answers.

Extending the skill: Find other comic strips or cartoons that require readers to make inferences. Help students read them and discover the inferences.

Talk About It To illustrate the discussion, invite students to bring to class examples of items or customs that their cultural group has contributed to the American way of life. Bring your own examples, too.

Write About It: Write Your Autobiography Read the introduction.

A. Have students answer the questions and add other information if they wish. They may want to list some of the important events in their life—getting a driver's license, marriage, births of children, and so on.

B. Have students complete the sentence starters and add other information if they wish. Remind them to write in complete sentences. Invite students to share their autobiographies with a partner or small group.

Word Work: The Suffix -ion Review the definitions of *prefix, root,* and *suffix.* Read the introductory paragraphs and the examples aloud.

Point out that when *-ion* is added to a root that ends in the letters *t* or *s,* the syllables *-tion* and *-sion* are formed. Both of these syllables are pronounced "shun." Point out that when they come to an unfamiliar word that ends in *-tion* or *-sion,* they should pronounce the ending "shun." (If students are confused by the difference between *-ion* and *-tion/-sion,* explain that a suffix is a division of meaning based on how words are formed. A syllable, on the other hand, is a division of sound or pronunciation based on one vowel sound per syllable.) Discuss the examples and ask students to suggest other examples. List them on the board.

Discuss how adding *-ion* usually changes the way a word is used. Discuss the examples and ask students to suggest others.

A–C. Read the directions with students and have them do the exercises independently. For A, be sure they know that they sometimes have to drop the final *e* before adding the suffix. For B, remind them that they may have to add a final *e* to the root after splitting the word.

Word Work extension: Use PCM 9. Ask students to add the suffix *-ion* to as many roots as they can. Point out that sometimes extra letters are added before *-ion,* as in *transportation.* List their words on the board.

More Practice: *Voyager 2 Workbook* p. 36

Have students fill out copies of PCM 13.

Lesson 12 (pp. 108–113)

Learning Goals Discuss the learning goals.

Before You Read Read and discuss the background material on the two poems. Ask if anyone has walked down a Manhattan sidewalk or has seen the movie or stage version of *South Pacific.*

Using PCM 12, show students the location of New York City on the map. Explain that Manhattan is in the center of the city. Then, on a world map or globe, locate some of the island groups in the South Pacific Ocean.

Ask students to share and discuss their examples of people acting with respect or from prejudice.

Key Words See Lesson 1 notes.

Use the Strategy Tell students that they will use their prior knowledge to better understand the two poems in this lesson. Students should recall what they know about the elements of rhyme, rhythm, and repetition in poetry and listen for these elements as they read each poem.

"Manhattan" and "You've Got to Be Carefully Taught" Discuss the picture. Read "Manhattan" aloud. Then do a paired reading with students. Accentuate the rhythm as you read:

‿ / ‿ ‿ ‿ / ‿ ‿ ‿ / ‿ ‿ ‿ /

There's A - sia on the A - ven - ue and Eur - ope on the street.

Discuss the check-in at the end of the poem.

Next read "You've Got to Be Carefully Taught" aloud, followed by a paired reading. Again, accentuate the rhythm. Finally, have students read the poem aloud individually or in small groups. Discuss the check-in. Explain that even though the poems are quite short, they both have a powerful message.

After You Read See Lesson 1 notes.

Talk About It To extend the discussion, ask how the pattern of passing prejudice from one generation to the next might be broken.

Extending the reading: Play a recording of the song "You've Got to Be Carefully Taught" for the class. Have students compare and contrast the experiences of reading the song and hearing it. If possible, have students watch the movie *South Pacific* on videotape.

Think About It: Identify Rhyme, Rhythm, and Repetition Read the first paragraph, which reviews three elements of poetry—rhyme, rhythm, and repetition. Ask students to give examples of each element.

Practice With the exception of number 3, have students complete the activities as independently as possible. For number 3, have the class read "Manhattan" and "You've Got to Be Carefully Taught" aloud and clap the rhythm of each poem together.

Extending the skill: Have students analyze a favorite song, identifying the elements of rhyme, rhythm, and repetition.

Write About It: Write a Poem Read and discuss the introduction.

A. Suggest that students think of a person they know of another race, religion, or culture. Then have students list their similarities and differences.

B. Have students add their ideas to create the poem "We Are Two People." Remind them to use their prewriting notes. Tell students that, if they prefer, they can write their own poems without using the frame provided. Ask volunteers to share their poems.

More Practice: *Voyager 2 Workbook* p. 38

Have students fill out copies of PCM 13.

Writing Skills Mini-Lesson: Compound Sentences (p. 114)

Read the introduction. Explain the difference between a simple sentence and a compound sentence (two simple sentences joined by *and* or *but*).

1. Explain the first rule. Read the example and suggest other examples such as *"We come to class, and we study hard."* Help students identify the subject and verb in each part of the sentence.

2. Read and discuss the second rule. Read the examples, and give others, such as *"Kim is tall, but I am short"* or *"We go to the same school, and we live in the same neighborhood."*

Practice When students feel comfortable with these rules, have them do the rewriting exercise independently on a separate piece of paper. Have them check their work with a partner or small group, date it, and put it in their working folders.

More Practice: *Voyager 2 Workbook* p. 39

Unit 4 Review (pp. 115–116)

Follow the process described in Unit 1. As students edit their writing, have them check that they have followed all the rules in the Writing Skills section of the Reference Handbook, page 126 of *Voyager 2*. Have students date their writing and put it in their working folders.

Extending the theme: To extend the theme "Celebrate Differences," ask students to imagine they are on a committee that is trying to bring people of various cultures together in the community. Have them discuss ways that people from different cultures could get to know each other better. One suggestion might be a cultural awareness day that includes dance, food, and music from each country.

More Practice: *Voyager 2 Workbook* p. 41

▶ *Final Note:* Review with students the copies of PCM 13 that they have placed in their working folders. Ask what additional help they think they need with material from the three lessons and the Writing Skills Mini-Lesson in Unit 4. Discuss possible ways of meeting those needs.

Skills Review (pp. 117–121)

When students have finished Unit 4, have them complete the Skills Review. Explain that this review will help them evaluate their reading and writing progress. Encourage them to evaluate their progress by checking their answers against those given on page 120. They can use the Evaluation Chart on page 121 to identify any skill areas they need to work on further. Meet with individual students to go over their results. Be sure that students complete the right side of the Student Interest Inventory on pages 6–7. Have them compare their answers to those they gave prior to beginning *Voyager 2* (see "Using the Skills Review," p. 14, and "Using the Student Interest Inventory," p. 13).

Alternative Assessment: Follow the instructions on PCM 14: Tips for Preparing a Progress Portfolio to help students evaluate the material in their working folders and assemble their Progress Portfolios. Then use PCM 15: Portfolio Conference Questionnaire to conduct an evaluation conference with each student.

Voyager 3 Teacher's Notes

Pre-Assessment

Before you begin Unit 1 with students, have them complete the Student Interest Inventory and the Skills Preview at the beginning of *Voyager 3* (see "Using the Student Interest Inventory" and "Using the Skills Preview," pp. 13–14).

In addition to *Voyager 3,* students will need
- folders in which to keep their work in progress

and their finished work (see "Working Folders," p. 7)
- a spiral-bound or three-ring notebook to use as a personal dictionary (see "Personal Dictionaries," pp. 16–17)
- a spiral-bound or three-ring notebook to use as a personal spelling list (see p. 20)

▶ Unit 1: Great Expectations

Part of Unit	Voyager 3 pages	TRG pages	Workbook pages
Overview	11	43	
Lesson 1	12 – 17	43 – 44	4
Lesson 2	18 – 25	44 – 45	5 – 6
Lesson 3	26 – 33	45 – 47	7 – 8
Writing Skills Mini-Lesson	34	47	9 – 10
Unit 1 Review	35 – 36	47	11 – 13

Student Objectives

Reading
- Read a song, a story, and a biography.
- Practice the strategies of using prior experience, predicting story features, and empathizing.
- Identify theme, understand plot, and find main idea and details.

Writing
- Write a song, a story, and a paragraph.

Speaking and Listening
- Read aloud, discuss, and interview.

Word Attack and Mechanics
- Use context clues to determine word meaning.
- Recognize compound words.
- Write compound sentences.

▶ Unit 1 PCMs
PCM 1: Cursive Handwriting
PCM 2: Cursive Handwriting Practice
PCM 3: Plot Map

PCM 4: Main Idea and Details Organizer
PCM 7: Using a Dictionary
PCM 11: Writing Starters
PCM 12: Map of the United States
PCM 13: Student Progress Tracking Sheet

▶ **Cursive Writing PCMs** For students who need to learn cursive writing, introduce it using PCM 1. Suggest that they work on four or five letters per lesson, first tracing over the guidelines on the PCM, then writing each letter on a copy of PCM 2B at least 10 times. Students who only need a review can use PCM 1 to practice letters they need to work on and then use PCM 2A and B to practice anything they want to write in cursive. Model the words and sentences they choose to learn on PCM 2B for them.

▶ **Personal Dictionaries and Spelling Lists**
Encourage students to add words they would like to learn to their dictionaries and spelling lists during each lesson in Unit 1 (see above).

Unit 1 Overview (p. 11)

The overview introduces the theme "Great Expectations." Discuss the collage of pictures. Tell students that each of the selections in the unit is represented in the collage. Read the overview aloud, and then conduct a paired reading (see "Working with Adult Emerging Readers," pp. 16–18). Discuss students' responses to the questions in the first paragraph.

Be an Active Reader Explain that as they read, "active" readers think about the information they are reading and try to figure out words or ideas they don't understand. Encourage students to mark things they don't understand with a question mark and to underline unknown words. After they have finished an entire selection, they can reread the marked sections to see if they now make sense.

Lesson 1 (pp. 12–17)

Learning Goals Read the learning goals aloud. Explain that Lesson 1 will focus on these goals.

Before You Read Read and discuss the first paragraph. Read the directions for the activity. Ask students to think about workers, homeless people, and children and to consider what would make their lives better. The group might brainstorm to generate ideas. Have students write their own answers.

Key Words The underlined words are important to the meaning of the reading. Have students read the sentences and try to figure out the meaning of each key word using context clues. Write the key words on the board. Ask students to read them aloud and to write words they want to learn in their personal dictionaries.

Use the Strategy Read the text aloud and discuss it. Encourage students to practice the strategy of using their personal experience to better understand the reading. Explain that active readers add their own experience to the information that they are reading to increase understanding. The check-ins within the reading selection also remind students to apply the strategy as they read.

"It Could Be a Wonderful World" Discuss the picture. Follow one of the strategies outlined in "Working with the Reading Selections" on page 14. Encourage students to mark the text as explained in "Be an Active Reader" on page 11. Be sure students use the check-ins to help them apply the strategy of using their experience. Discuss how the song is similar to a poem (it has groups of lines called stanzas, and rhyme and rhythm patterns). Point out that the repeated stanza is called the "chorus" or "refrain." Ask if students know any refrains from other songs.

After You Read

A–B. Have students reread sections they marked and look back at words they underlined. Discuss any they still don't understand. Remind them to add words they want to learn to their personal dictionaries.

C. Have students work as independently as possible. Encourage them to look back at the reading to review details or to confirm their answers when necessary. Discuss their responses.

Talk About It Students should be able to explain why they consider the problem they chose to be more important than the others. Have students brainstorm to generate many possible solutions. Encourage students to write their responses, date their writing, and place it in their working folders.

Extending the reading: Find another song or a poem with the theme "Great Expectations." One option might be "The New Colossus" by Emma Lazarus, which is inscribed on the Statue of Liberty, specifically the section that begins "Give me your tired, your poor." Have students practice reading it in pairs to work on fluency and rhythm.

Think About It: Find the Theme Ask students to read the first two paragraphs about theme. Discuss how a theme is the author's central message. Point out that the topics listed are broad, general concepts that concern many people. Themes are specific opinions or statements related to such topics.

Read the two questions that lead to discovering the theme of a piece of writing.

Read question 1 of the matching exercise. Ask students to explain why *c* is the best choice. Have students match the remaining themes and topics. Discuss their answers. Also discuss using the process of elimination in this type of exercise. Tell students to first match themes and topics they are sure of and then make the remaining matches.

Practice Students should complete the activity independently. Remind them that the topic is usually a word or short phrase. If necessary, help them identify the topic by looking for words repeated in the paragraph or a topic sentence.

Extending the skill: Have students work in pairs to find the theme of the poem or song you introduced in "Extending the reading." Ask students to explain how they identified the topic and the theme. Discuss their strategies.

Write About It: Write a Song Read the first two paragraphs and the song with students. Ask them to name the rhyming words. Then have them reread the poem while clapping to the beat.

A. Tell students they are brainstorming and should not worry about rhyme or rhythm at this point. Every idea should be accepted and recorded.

B. Encourage students to read the lines aloud, trying different words and listening to the rhythm and rhyme. Students should each write a complete song in their books whether they created it on their own or with a group (see "Working with Adult Emerging Writers," pp.18–20).

More Practice: *Voyager 3 Workbook* p. 4 The workbook exercises are designed to be done independently and should not require teacher input.

Have students fill out copies of PCM 13 to include in their working folders.

Lesson 2 (pp. 18–25)

Learning Goals Read the learning goals aloud. Explain that Lesson 2 will focus on these goals.

Before You Read Read the first paragraph and the directions. Explain that students should check all of the features they think they will find in the story.

Key Words See Lesson 1 notes.

Use the Strategy Tell students that they will use the strategy of predicting story features to better understand the reading. Explain that predicting keeps a reader actively involved. If we look for features we expect to find in the story, we will recognize them as we read and understand the story better.

"The New Boss" Discuss the picture. Follow one of the strategies outlined in "Working with the Reading Selections" on page 14. If students are unfamiliar with factory environments, they may need background information on assembly lines and production goals. Be sure students use the check-ins as reminders to apply the strategy of predicting features.

After You Read See Lesson 1 notes.

Talk About It Ask students to back up their opinions with details from the story. They should cite specific actions by Kim and the workers that might predict her success or failure.

Extending the reading

1. Refer back to the features listed in "Before You Read" on page 18. Ask if students think the story included "facts about the world." Students might mention that some male workers feel resentment toward female supervisors. Ask students if they can tell what the writer thinks about the story. Explain that writers usually don't state their opinions directly, but the way they tell a story often gives clues about their beliefs. Have students discuss how they think this author feels about equality between men and women on the job. Then ask students what they think about the issue.

2. Ask students to think about their own job goals and expectations. Help them list their goals, putting the most important one first.

Think About It: Understand the Plot Introduce plot by asking volunteers to tell the story line of a TV show or movie. Explain that story plots usually follow the same general pattern of rising action, climax, and falling action.

Read the explanation and the definitions. Then read and discuss the three parts of the plot of "The New Boss." Show how the plot map pictures the story. Point out that the rising action line is long because it takes up most of the story. The climax happens quickly, and the ending, or falling action, is usually short.

Practice Have students complete the practice independently and discuss their responses.

Extending the skill: Find a very short story with a well-defined plot, such as an anecdote or a fable. Provide copies so students can follow along as you read aloud. Have them use PCM 3 and work in pairs to complete plot maps. Have students date their plot maps and put them in their working folders.

Write About It: Write a Story Read and discuss the first paragraph and the list of experiences.

A. Tell students to write brief summaries of their experiences by answering the questions. The climax is listed first because it is often the most memorable part. Have students transfer their summaries to the plot maps. Since space is limited, you may have to show students how to write only the important words.

B. Help students construct stories based on their maps. Encourage them to add whatever details they remember. Have students date their writing and put it in their working folders.

Word Work: Using Context Clues to Figure Out Word Meaning Read the first paragraph. Explain that experienced readers use context clues more than any other strategy to identify unfamiliar words and figure out meanings. Using this strategy, when they encounter an unfamiliar word, they continue reading and try to figure out the meaning from the rest of the sentence or paragraph. They can look up the word later to confirm the guess.

Read and discuss the tips. Ask students how the context in each example gives clues to meaning.

Practice Read the directions for the exercise. As students choose their answers, have them identify the clue words and find a similar example in the tips.

Word Work extension: Use PCM 7 to introduce or review dictionary use. Explain that experienced readers check their guess about what a word is or means in the dictionary. If necessary, review and practice alphabetical order. Help students become familiar with the dictionary by doing some of the activities suggested on the PCM. Encourage dictionary use whenever appropriate.

More Practice: *Voyager 3 Workbook* p. 5

Have students fill out copies of PCM 13 to include in their working folders.

Lesson 3 (pp. 26–33)

Learning Goals Read the learning goals aloud. Explain that Lesson 3 will focus on these goals.

Before You Read Read the first paragraph. Ask students what they already know about Shaquille O'Neal. Discuss the meaning of the phrase *measure up,* and ask students to predict what the story will be about based on the title.

Read the directions for the activity and allow students time to complete it. If necessary, help them write their answers.

Key Words See Lesson 1 notes.

Use the Strategy Tell students that they will use the strategy of understanding how another person feels to better grasp the reading. Explain that to use this strategy, it helps to imagine themselves in a similar situation.

"Shaq Measures Up" Discuss the picture. Follow one of the strategies outlined in "Working with the Reading Selections" on page 14. Be sure students use the check-ins as reminders to apply the strategy of empathizing. If students are unfamiliar with terms such as *NBA, draft,* and other basketball words, remind them to underline the words and try to use context clues to figure them out. Point out that we don't always need to understand every word in what we read in order to understand it. Discuss the meanings of unfamiliar terms after students finish reading.

After You Read See Lesson 1 notes.

Talk About It Extend the discussion by asking, *"How did Shaq's childhood prepare him to handle adult pressures? Do you think children who play organized sports are under too much pressure to perform?"* Ask students to explain their opinions.

Extending the reading

1. Ask students to form pairs or small groups and list the skills, personal qualities, and support from others that it took for Shaq to achieve his goals. Then ask students to think about their own academic or career goals, and make lists of specific skills, personal strengths, and resources they might need to accomplish them.

2. Use PCM 11, activity 2. Ask students to complete the sentences about "Shaq Measures Up." Have students date their writing and put it in their working folders.

3. Point out Louisiana, where Shaquille O'Neal went to college, on PCM 12. Have students find Florida, where he first played professional basketball. Ask if anyone knows where Orlando is (near the center of the state). (*Note:* Have students keep their copy of PCM 12 for future reference.)

Think About It: Find the Main Idea and Details Use an everyday example to introduce the concept. For instance, pick a story out of the newspaper and tell what it is about in general—the main idea. Then add the details. Explain why it is important to understand the main idea: if we remember Shaq's birthday but can't tell how he achieved success, we've missed the point.

Read and discuss the introduction and the example paragraph. Point out that sometimes the author states the main idea in the beginning, as in this paragraph, but this isn't always true.

Ask students to read the supporting details and answer the question. Discuss their answers.

Discuss how the graphic organizer illustrates the structure of a paragraph, with the main idea spanning all the details, and the details supporting the main idea.

Practice Students should complete the practice independently. Discuss their responses.

Extending the skill: Use PCM 4. Find an article with a clear main idea and details, such as a news article from *News for You,* the newspaper published by New Readers Press. Have students read the article and identify the main idea and details. Then have them fill them in on the organizer on the PCM. Have students date their work and put it in their working folders.

Write About It: Write a Paragraph Read the first paragraph. Review the definition and structure of a paragraph in "Think About It" on page 30.

A. Refer students to their answers in "Before You Read" on page 26 and ask them to think of other strategies they have used when under pressure. Have them make notes on the organizer.

B. Help students use their notes to write a paragraph with complete sentences. Have students date their writing and put it in their working folders.

Talk About It Help students write questions to use in their interviews. Tell them to leave space between the questions so they can take notes on the answers. Students can complete the graphic organizer on PCM 4 whether or not they decide to write a paragraph.

Word Work: Recognizing Words Read and briefly discuss the strategies for decoding longer words. Explain that this page introduces all the topics covered in "Word Work" pages in the book, but this lesson is specifically about compound words.

Read and discuss the reminder. Then read the definition of a compound word and the tip. Explain that the meaning of a compound word may often be found by combining the meanings of the two smaller words. Demonstrate using the examples.

Read the directions for the exercise. Help students if necessary. Ask them to find one word among the words in the exercise that doesn't have the same meaning as its component words (*understand*).

Word Work extension: For extra dictionary practice, have students find the five Practice words in their dictionary.

More Practice: *Voyager 3 Workbook* p. 7

Have students fill out copies of PCM 13 to include in their working folders.

Writing Skills Mini-Lesson: Compound Sentences (p. 34)

To successfully complete this mini-lesson, students must understand the concept of a complete sentence and be able to recognize subjects and verbs. Review these concepts if necessary.

Read the first paragraph. Point out that just as a compound word is made up of two words, a compound sentence is made up of two sentences. Each of the parts of a compound sentence could stand on its own as a complete thought.

1–3. Read the rules and examples. Write additional examples on the board, pointing out subjects, verbs, and connecting words. Be sure students understand how to use the different connecting words. Give examples using the wrong connecting word (*but* instead of *so,* for instance) and ask students to supply the correct word.

Practice writing compound sentences by having one student suggest the first complete thought, another to suggest a connecting word, and a third to provide the second complete thought.

Practice Have students do the exercise independently or in pairs and then share their sentences with the group. Check to make sure students place the comma before the connecting word. Have students date their sentences and put them in their working folders.

Extending the skill: Have students find some compound sentences in the story "Shaq Measures Up." Also have them create compound sentences by joining some of the simple sentences from the story.

More Practice: *Voyager 3 Workbook* p. 9

Unit 1 Review (pp. 35–36)

Explain that this review will help students evaluate what they have learned in Unit 1.

Reading Review Have students complete the questions independently. Discuss their responses.

Writing Process Read the opening paragraph and the list of drafts students wrote in Unit 1. Then turn to page 128 in *Voyager 3*. Read and discuss the five steps of the writing process. Explain that students have already completed steps 1 and 2 for the three pieces they wrote in Unit 1. Help students locate the drafts they want to work with further. Work with students as they revise, edit, and create a final draft.

To help students with the revising step, go over the specific point listed for that type of draft. When they get to the editing step, remind students to check that compound sentences are written and punctuated correctly. Have students date their final drafts and put them in their working folders.

Extending the theme: To extend the theme of "Great Expectations," use PCM 11. Reluctant writers might use one of the sentence starters in activity 1 to write about an expectation, hope, or goal they have. Students more comfortable with writing might try to write a paragraph in response to one of the statements in activity 3. Have students date their writing and put it in their working folders.

More Practice: *Voyager 3 Workbook* p. 11

▶ *Final Note:* Review with students the copies of PCM 13 that they have placed in their working folders. Ask what additional help they think they need with the material from the three lessons and the Writing Skills Mini-Lesson in Unit 1. Discuss possible ways of meeting those needs.

▶ Unit 2: Across Generations

Part of Unit	Voyager 3 pages	TRG pages	Workbook pages
Overview	37	48	
Lesson 4	38 – 43	48 – 49	14
Lesson 5	44 – 51	49 – 51	15 – 16
Lesson 6	52 – 59	51 – 52	17 – 18
Writing Skills Mini-Lesson	60	52	19 – 20
Unit 2 Review	61 – 62	52	21 – 23

Student Objectives

Reading
- Read a poem, a journal entry, and a story.
- Practice the strategies of using prior experience, predicting content, and empathizing.
- Find the theme, draw conclusions, and understand character.

Writing
- Write a poem, a journal entry, and a character description.

Speaking and Listening
- Read aloud, discuss, and retell.

Word Attack and Mechanics
- Recognize prefixes, roots, and suffixes.
- Write complex sentences.

▶ Unit 2 PCMs
PCM 1: Cursive Handwriting
PCM 2: Cursive Handwriting Practice
PCM 3: Plot Map
PCM 5: Character Web
PCM 6: Story Frame
PCM 7: Using a Dictionary
PCM 8: Common Prefixes
PCM 9: Common Roots
PCM 10: Common Suffixes
PCM 13: Student Progress Tracking Sheet

▶ **Cursive Writing PCMs** Use PCM 1 and 2B with students who are continuing to practice four or five letters per lesson. Use PCM 2A and B with students who need practice writing their names and sentences. Write practice words and sentences on the board as models.

▶ **Personal Dictionaries and Spelling Lists**
Encourage students to add words they would like to learn to their dictionaries and spelling lists during each lesson in Unit 2 (see p. 42).

Unit 2 Overview (p. 37)

The overview introduces the theme "Across Generations." Discuss the collage of pictures. Tell students the readings in the unit are all represented in the collage. Ask, *"How many generations are in your family? Do you have friends or neighbors in generations other than your own?"* Discuss students' responses. Read the overview together. Discuss the two questions in the last paragraph.

Be an Active Reader See Unit 1 notes.

Lesson 4 (pp. 38–43)

Learning Goals Discuss the learning goals.

Before You Read Read and discuss the first paragraph and the directions for the activity. Tell students that there are no right or wrong answers; they should mark what is true about their own families. If students don't have much information about earlier generations of their families, suggest that they use their general knowledge of the past.

Key Words See Lesson 1 notes.

Use the Strategy Read the text aloud. Tell students that, as they did in Lesson 1, they will draw on their personal experiences to help them understand the poem. Encourage them to apply the strategy by comparing the grandmothers in the poem with their own older relatives.

"Lineage" Read the poem aloud; then do a paired reading with students. Finally, let them read the poem aloud on their own, paying attention to repeated words and phrases, and to the rhythm, which is irregular.

After You Read See Lesson 1 notes.

Talk About It Students may base their discussion on information about their own grandparents or their knowledge of life in the past. List their responses on the board under the headings "Easier" and "Harder."

Extending the reading: Have students discuss the following questions in pairs or small groups: *"If the poet had been writing about grandfathers, how would the poem be different? What words would be different if you were describing grandfathers? What words would be the same?"* Have them brainstorm a list of words to describe grandfathers. Discuss the results.

Think About It: Find the Theme Read and discuss the first four paragraphs.

Read the sample paragraph and work through the process of identifying topic and theme. Discuss how you arrived at the answers: by looking for a topic sentence and noting repeated words and ideas.

Practice Have students read the paragraph and the poem and answer the questions independently. If necessary, provide help or allow students to work in pairs. Assure them that the wording of answers may vary.

Extending the skill: Find a short story with an intergenerational theme. Read it or have volunteers take turns reading it. Have students identify the general topic and discuss the theme.

Write About It: Write a Poem Read the first paragraph.
A. Read the directions and give examples of names and memories from your own family. If necessary, help students write their ideas on the lines.
B. If students have trouble, suggest that they use "Lineage" or "Single Father" (p. 42) as a model. Some students may find it easier to

focus on one family member.

It is important that students read their poems aloud to hear the sounds of the words and the rhythm of the lines. However, some students may not want others to hear their poems. Provide a private area for students who wish to read quietly. Have students date their writing and put it in their working folders.

Writing extension: Students might enjoy working on a group poem entitled "Family," for which each member of the group contributes one line.

More Practice: *Voyager 3 Workbook* p. 14

Have students fill out copies of PCM 13 to include in their working folders.

Lesson 5 (pp. 44–51)

Learning Goals Discuss the learning goals.

Before You Read Read the introduction and directions, and ask students to complete the activity on their own. Discuss their answers.

Key Words See Lesson 1 notes.

Use the Strategy Tell students that they will use the strategy of predicting to help them understand the reading in this lesson. Remind students that making predictions keeps them involved in their reading and makes them want to read on to see if they have predicted correctly.

"A Mother's Gift" Discuss the picture. Follow one of the strategies outlined in "Working with the Reading Selections" on page 14. Be sure students use the check-ins as reminders to apply the strategy of predicting. Point out that the dates show the different days on which Tina wrote in her journal.

After You Read See Lesson 1 notes.

Talk About It Students should explain not only what the statement means, but what it implies about our actions. Ask, *"If children are the future, what should we—parents, teachers, and society as a whole—do differently or better?"* Ask students to be specific. List their responses.

Extending the reading: Discuss the information and feelings Tina chose to record for her child. Then ask students to think about what they would like the next generation of their family to know about them. Ask each one to write one or two things to share with their children. Students who don't plan to have children could choose to share their ideas with younger family members. Students may share their writing or keep it private.

Think About It: Draw Conclusions Ask students what it means to draw a conclusion. Tell them that when we draw a conclusion, we come to a decision about something, using information that we haven't been told directly.

Read and discuss the explanation and the example. Point out that it can be risky to draw conclusions based on incomplete information. Ask, *"What if we did not know the couple wore wedding rings? Would it be safe to conclude they are a family with married parents?"*

Work through the guided practice with students. Have them write their own conclusion on the line. Ask them to support it with information from the list.

Practice Have students complete the exercise as independently as possible. For "yes" answers, help them write explanations of their conclusions. Discuss their answers. Students should also be able to explain their thinking if they answer "no."

Extending the skill: Have students turn back to the story "The New Boss" in Lesson 2 and reread the last paragraph. Ask students to draw conclusions about the workers' reactions. Say, *"How does Todd feel now? Do the other workers support him or Kim? What evidence do you have to support your conclusions?"*

Write About It: Write a Journal Entry Read and discuss the first paragraph.
A. Explain that because a journal is not usually meant for others to read, the writer doesn't usually prewrite a journal entry. Instead, the writer usually thinks of a topic and writes thoughts as they come to mind. Invite students to think of a topic and jot it down.

B. Suggest that students use Tina's entries as a model.

Word Work: Prefixes and Roots The activities on this page are challenging. Allow plenty of time to introduce and practice this word recognition strategy.

Read the introduction and explain that identifying prefixes and roots is another strategy for recognizing unfamiliar words. Experienced readers break longer words into parts to read and figure out their meaning.

Read and discuss the chart. Be sure students understand what each column contains and how to read across the rows. Give additional examples of words that use the prefixes, such as *antipoverty, misplace, prepaid, transplant.* Ask students to suggest others and list them.

Read the tip aloud. Demonstrate with one of the words in the chart. Point out that not all long words are made up of prefixes and roots, but many are. Also note that many roots are not whole words.

Practice
A. Read the directions and have students complete the exercise. Discuss the meanings of the words. Tell students that prefixes and roots may give a clue to meaning, but may not always provide an exact definition. Model using the dictionary to confirm definitions. Tell students that they can use their knowledge of prefixes and roots along with phonics and context clues to recognize words and figure out their meanings.
B. Have students work alone or in pairs to complete this activity. They should come up with at least one word for each prefix and root. Encourage them to use the dictionary. List all the words students generate on the board. Students should add words they didn't think of to their own lists. Have them date their work and put it in their working folders.

Word Work extension
1. When students understand the concept of prefixes, begin using PCMs 8 and 9. Read the first

prefix on PCM 8, its meaning, and the example. Then form another word by matching the prefix to a root on PCM 9. Ask students to match another root with the prefix. List their words on the board. Repeat with two or three more prefixes. Continue working with prefixes and roots this way in subsequent lessons. Have students date their work and put it in their working folders.

2. Continue to familiarize students with dictionary use by having them use the words in exercise A to do activities on PCM 7.

More Practice: *Voyager 3 Workbook* p. 15

Have students fill out copies of PCM 13 to include in their working folders.

Lesson 6 (pp. 52–59)

Learning Goals Discuss the learning goals.

Before You Read Read and discuss the first paragraph. Explain that thinking about the father-son relationship will prepare students to better understand the characters' feelings.

Have students complete the activity and discuss their responses.

Key Words See Lesson 1 notes.

Use the Strategy Review the strategy of understanding how another person feels that was introduced in Lesson 3.

"Suspect" Discuss the picture. Follow one of the strategies outlined in "Working with the Reading Selections" on page 14. Be sure students use the check-ins as reminders to apply the strategy of empathizing. Remind students that in a story, a new paragraph begins each time a different character begins to speak and quotation marks enclose the words a character speaks.

After You Read See Lesson 1 notes.

Talk About It If students need help retelling the story, suggest they first list key events in sequence or draw a plot map using PCM 3. Ask them to explain why they think Jack did or did not handle the situation well.

Extending the reading: Review the skill of drawing conclusions introduced in Lesson 5. Discuss these questions: *"Do we know enough to draw conclusions about Brian's guilt or innocence? What explanations might account for Brian's presence at the crime scene?"* Have students offer different endings for the story.

Think About It: Understand Character Read the first paragraph. Have students complete the checklist.

Read and discuss the information about Jack. Remind students that all this information is in the story. Explain that details we read about characters can help us draw conclusions about them. Read and discuss the guided practice question.

Practice Have students complete the exercise independently and discuss their answers. Remind them to look for context clues to define the phrase "out of character" in the first question.

Extending the skill
1. Use PCM 5. Demonstrate how to make a character web by completing one about Jack Tanner. Then ask students to make a character web about Brian Tanner, using information from the story and the description in Practice on page 57. Have students date their work and put it in their working folders.
2. Use PCM 6 to help students summarize the main story elements of "Suspect." Students may refer to the story to complete the story frame. Have students date their work and put it in their working folders.

Write About It: Describe a Character Read the first paragraph.
A. Explain that both possible descriptions of Susan Tanner include the kind of information we learned about Jack Tanner. Students should choose one of the descriptions and try to imagine Susan. Then they can add one or two other details that are "in character" for Susan.
B. Tell students to begin by writing complete sentences using the descriptions they chose in Part A. They should include sentences about the details they have added. Have students date their writing and put it in their working folders.

Talk About It Tell students to use what they learned about Brian in the description on page 57 in making their predictions. Their predictions about whether Susan would be supportive will depend on which description of her they chose to write about.

Word Work: Prefixes, Roots, and Suffixes Review what students learned about prefixes and roots in Lesson 5. Then read and discuss the first two paragraphs and examples.

Explain that figuring out unfamiliar words can be easier if you can recognize word parts. Point out that some long words have one or more prefixes, a root, and one or more suffixes; some words have just a prefix or a suffix and the root; some long words aren't made up of these word parts at all. Read the tip and demonstrate it using *predictable*. Help students read the chart.

Practice

A. Read the directions and work through the first two words as examples. Have students do the rest independently.

B. Read the directions. Students may work independently or in pairs. Remind them that they may need to add, change, or delete letters to form some words. Use *expectation* as an example. Point out that the *s* is dropped from the root *spect* and *at* is added before the suffix *ion*. Encourage students to use the dictionary. Create a master list of all the actual words students generate. Have students date their work and put it in their working folders.

Word Work extension: If students understand the concepts of prefixes, roots, and suffixes, continue using PCMs 8 and 9 and begin using PCM 10. Follow the process described in Lesson 5, pages 50–51. Have students use the dictionary to confirm the spelling of the words they form.

More Practice: *Voyager 3 Workbook* p. 17

Have students fill out copies of PCM 13 to include in their working folders.

Writing Skills Mini-Lesson: Complex Sentences (p. 60)

Review the concepts of complete sentences, subjects, and verbs. Introduce the term *clause*.

Read and discuss the first paragraph and the example.

1–2. Read and discuss the definitions of independent and dependent clauses and the examples. Give additional examples and ask students for other examples.

3. Read and discuss the rule about clauses having subjects and verbs.

Practice

On the board, write three or four dependent clauses like those in the exercise. Ask students to compose independent clauses to make them complex sentences. Have them identify the subjects and verbs in each clause. When students are comfortable with the format of the exercise, allow them to complete it independently. Have students date their work and put it in their working folders.

More Practice: *Voyager 3 Workbook* p. 19

Unit 2 Review (pp. 61–62)

Follow the process described in Unit 1. As students edit their writing, have them check that compound and complex sentences are written and punctuated correctly. Have students date their writing and put it in their working folders.

Extending the theme: To extend the theme "Across Generations," have students use PCM 5 to make a character web about a parent, grandparent, child, or grandchild. Encourage students to add pictures and write character descriptions or short biographies based on their webs.

More Practice: *Voyager 3 Workbook* p. 21

▶ *Final Note:* Review with students the copies of PCM 13 that they have placed in their working folders. Ask what additional help they think they need with material from the three lessons and the Writing Skills Mini-Lesson in Unit 2. Discuss possible ways of meeting those needs.

▶ Unit 3: Voices for Justice

Part of Unit	Voyager 3 pages	TRG pages	Workbook pages
Overview	63	53	
Lesson 7	64 – 71	53 – 55	24 – 25
Lesson 8	72 – 79	55 – 56	26 – 27
Lesson 9	80 – 85	56 – 57	28
Writing Skills Mini-Lesson	86	57	29 – 30
Unit 3 Review	87 – 88	57	31 – 33

Student Objectives

Reading
- Read a story, a biography, and two speeches.
- Practice the strategies of predicting content, using prior knowledge, and empathizing.
- Identify setting, understand the main idea and details, and identify viewpoint.

Writing
- Describe a setting, write an interview, and write a paragraph expressing a viewpoint.

Speaking and Listening
- Retell, interview, and discuss.

Word Attack and Mechanics
- Divide words into syllables.
- Write complex sentences.

▶ Unit 3 PCMs
PCM 4: Main Idea and Details Organizer
PCM 5: Character Web
PCM 6: Story Frame
PCM 11: Writing Starters
PCM 12: Map of the United States
PCM 13: Student Progress Tracking Sheet

▶ Personal Dictionaries and Spelling Lists
Encourage students to add words they would like to learn to their dictionaries and spelling lists during each lesson in Unit 3 (see p. 42).

Unit 3 Overview (p. 63)

The overview introduces the theme "Voices for Justice." Discuss the collage of pictures and ask if students recognize Nelson Mandela or Chief Joseph. Ask, *"What do you think a person has to do to become a voice for justice?"* Discuss students' responses. Read the overview together. Discuss the questions in the last paragraph.

Be an Active Reader See Unit 1 notes.

Lesson 7 (pp. 64–71)

Learning Goals Discuss the learning goals.

Before You Read Read or have volunteers read the first two paragraphs. Have students discuss the questions in pairs or groups.

Read the directions for the activity and, if necessary, the checklist. Ask students to complete the checklist and discuss their predictions.

Key Words See Lesson 1 notes.

Use the Strategy Tell students that they will use the strategy of prediction, which they practiced in Lessons 2 and 5. Read the paragraph together.

"A Safe Place" Discuss the picture. Follow one of the strategies outlined in "Working with the Reading Selections" on page 14. Be sure students use the check-ins to help them apply the strategy of predicting.

After You Read See Lesson 1 notes.

Talk About It Point out to students that Jane lived with abuse for some time. Ask what made her able to withstand Mick's pleading this time. Have students list the factors that led to Jane's decision to stay at the shelter. Encourage them to deal with the complexity of this issue.

Extending the reading

1. Use PCM 11, activity 6. Ask students to think about Jane's decision and write about a decision they have had to make. Remind students to prewrite; if necessary, help them list and organize their ideas. Have students date their writing and put it in their working folders.

2. Use PCM 5. Have students make character webs for both Clara and Jane. Have them date their work and put it in their working folders.

Think About It: Identify Setting Read and discuss the first two paragraphs. Students can look back at the story to complete the sentences if they wish. Read the paragraph that gives the answers, and ask students to share any additional details that they imagined.

Discuss the next two paragraphs. Ask students to imagine details about the five settings listed. Have them list words and phrases that describe the feelings each setting might evoke. Have them compare their lists with a partner or small group.

Practice Have students complete the exercise independently.

Extending the skill: Have students use PCM 6 to summarize the setting, characters, and plot of "A Safe Place." Have students date their work and put it in their working folders.

More Practice: *Voyager 3 Workbook* p. 24

Write About It: Describe a Setting Read the introduction.

A. If necessary, help students fill in details about the setting they chose.

B. Have students use their prewriting ideas to complete the paragraph. They should add as many details as they can think of to help the reader picture and feel the setting. Have students share their work with a partner. Then have them date their writing and put it in their working folders.

Writing extension: Ask students to imagine a story titled "The Hiding Place." Have students work in pairs to rewrite the first three paragraphs of "A Safe Place" as the start of this story: Clara,

Jane's friend, lives alone. Clara lets Jane hide in her house, and both women are afraid. Help students replace the words that describe "A Safe Place" with ones that describe a fearful setting.

Word Work: Dividing Words into Syllables Read and discuss the first paragraph. Explain that dividing an unfamiliar word into syllables is another way to make it easier to read.

Read and discuss the tips and examples. Remind students that a final *e* after a consonant is usually silent. Therefore, the final *e* on *cooperate* does not indicate another syllable. Teach or review vowel pairs and vowel-consonant clusters as necessary.

Students may ask about the difference between syllables and the word parts they studied in Unit 2. Explain that prefixes, roots, and suffixes are divisions of meaning, while syllables are divisions of sound. Using syllables, words are divided by the way they are pronounced, with one vowel sound per syllable. Point out that the pronunciation guides in dictionaries divide words by syllables.

Practice Read the directions for the exercise. For known words, suggest that students count syllables by tapping to the "beat" of the word. Then they can divide the words, using the tips. For unfamiliar words, help students apply the tips to divide the words. Have them read each word one syllable at a time. Then have them pronounce the word normally.

Have students check and discuss their answers. Ask them to mark any words they do not recognize and look the words up in a dictionary. They should read the pronunciation guide and definitions and use the words in sentences. Encourage students to write words they want to learn in their personal dictionaries.

Point out that dividing words into syllables is often a difficult strategy to apply because it is not always clear where to divide an unfamiliar word. For example, the words *cartoon* and *cooperate* both include the *oo* spelling. Tell students that they should try dividing an unfamiliar word both ways, sound it out, and listen for a familiar word. Remind them that when reading they can use context clues, along with strategies like syllabication, to identify words and figure out meanings.

More Practice: *Voyager 3 Workbook* p. 24

Have students fill out copies of PCM 13.

Lesson 8 (pp. 72–79)

Learning Goals Discuss the learning goals.

Before You Read Read and discuss the introductory paragraph. Locate South Africa on a globe or world map.

Explain that the activities will help students recall what they already know about Nelson Mandela and South Africa. Read the directions for each activity and, if necessary, the facts in the checklist. Students should complete the activities independently.

Key Words See Lesson 1 notes.

Use the Strategy Tell students that they will apply the strategy of using what they know to better understand the reading. As we read, we recall what we have learned in school, from our own experience, from watching TV, and from talking to others. Explain that the more background knowledge they have about the topic, the better they will understand the reading.

"Voice of a People" Discuss the pictures. Preview the reading by asking students to read the subheads and captions before they read the whole piece. Explain that subheads provide a preview of the reading. Also remind students to pay attention to the subheads as they read. Subheads break up a long piece into sections. They show how the information is organized, and they help us predict. Be sure students use the check-ins to help them apply the strategy of using their knowledge.

After You Read See Lesson 1 notes.

Talk About It Students should understand that this saying referred to Nelson Mandela's government when it was very new. Ask them to draw comparisons between a newborn child and a new government. Challenge students to think of other things a

new government might be compared to, such as a machine that needs to be oiled and "broken in" or a new marriage.

Extending the reading: Check news magazines and newspapers, including *News for You,* the newspaper published by New Readers Press, for articles about South Africa or Nelson Mandela. Provide copies and read the article aloud as students follow along. Discuss the article, and ask students to identify what they already knew and what they learned from "Voice of a People."

Think About It: Understand the Main Idea and Details Read the first paragraph. Review the definition of main idea and supporting details introduced in Lesson 3. Show how the chart illustrates the relationship between the main idea and major details (subheads).

Practice Read the directions. Help students see the relationship between the main idea and the major details (subheads) of the article. Make sure they understand that the subheads are in turn the main ideas of the sections. Then have students fill in the blanks independently. They may look back at the story to check details.

Extending the skill: Use PCM 4 and the article about South Africa you chose for "Extending the reading." Have students complete the organizer. If the article is complex, divide it into sections and assign pairs of students one section each.

Write About It: Write an Interview Read and discuss the first paragraph.
A. If necessary, help students read the questions. Demonstrate how to take notes on answers.
B. Students can use the paragraph frame as a guide. Encourage them to add other information as well. Have students work as independently as possible, providing help if needed. Have students date their writing and put it in their working folders.

Writing extension: Use PCM 11, activity 7. Ask students to think about how Nelson Mandela's beliefs guided his actions. Then have them write about a time when they acted on one of their own beliefs. Help them with prewriting as necessary.

Have students date their writing and put it in their working folders.

Word Work: More Dividing Words into Syllables
Follow the process described in Lesson 7. Teach or review consonant blends and digraphs. Have students read the words in Tip 3 aloud with you, focusing on the pronunciation of the final syllable.

Review the three tips from Lesson 7. Then post all six tips and their examples for reference.

Practice Follow the suggestions in Lesson 7. Have students work through the first column in pairs. Discuss answers and the meanings of unknown words.

More Practice: *Voyager 3 Workbook* p. 26

Have students fill out copies of PCM 13.

Lesson 9 (pp. 80–85)

Learning Goals Discuss the learning goals.

Before You Read Read and discuss the first two paragraphs. Ask what students already know about the experiences of Native Americans in the 1800s.

Read the third paragraph and the statements aloud. Be sure students understand that the statements are opinions. They may agree or disagree with them. Let students answer independently. Tell them that the reading may support or make them rethink their opinions.

Key Words See Lesson 1 notes.

Use the Strategy Review the strategy of understanding how another person feels, practiced in Lessons 3 and 6.

"Let Me Be a Free Man" Discuss the picture. Follow one of the strategies outlined in "Working with the Reading Selections" on page 14. Explain the use of brackets and ellipses in quoted material. Brackets look like squared-off parentheses. They indicate that an editor or writer has added material that wasn't in the original, usually to make the meaning clearer. Ellipsis marks are three spaced periods. They let the reader know that something

from the original has been left out. Be sure students use the check-in to help them try to understand the chief's feelings.

To help students feel the power of this piece, read the speech aloud as you imagine Chief Joseph might have spoken it. You may also ask a volunteer to read it. Always allow students to read silently before asking them to read aloud.

After You Read See Lesson 1 notes.

Extension Have students use PCM 12 to find the Northwest region of the United States and the U.S.–Canada border.

Talk About It To guide discussion of the last two questions, give students copies of the Bill of Rights and help them list some of the freedoms guaranteed by this part of the U.S. Constitution. Ask if they think Chief Joseph's people were denied these freedoms.

Extending the reading: Ask each student to draw a picture, write a statement, or create a poem or song that expresses Chief Joseph's ideas and feelings about freedom or justice. Have students date their work and put it in their working folders.

Think About It: Identify Viewpoint Read the first paragraph and discuss the words *viewpoint, belief,* and *opinion*. Tell students that here, the words mean about the same thing. Say, *"Your opinion is what you believe to be true. Your beliefs and opinions help shape your viewpoint."*

Together, read, discuss, and summarize the examples of viewpoint and the forces that help determine viewpoint. Explain that to understand others, we must try to see things from their viewpoint, or perspective. To understand what we read, we often have to "try on" the writer's perspective—to put ourselves in his or her shoes.

Have students write their answers to the guided practice and discuss.

Practice Read the directions. Read the speech aloud, and then ask a volunteer to read it. Have students answer the questions independently and discuss their answers.

Extending the skill

1. Ask students to discuss the U.S. government's viewpoint, and why many white people wanted to keep the Native Americans on reservations. Then ask student volunteers to role-play a meeting between Chief Joseph and the president of the United States, where they present their viewpoints and argue their cases.

2. Encourage interested students to research Native American history during the 1800s or, more specifically, the stories of Chief Joseph and Sitting Bull. If possible, work with a librarian who can help students locate materials, or provide suitable resources yourself.

Write About It: Write Your Viewpoint Read the first paragraph.

A. Have students choose a topic about an unjust situation. Read the questions to be answered. Ask students to write a few words or phrases in answer to each question.

B. Suggest that students use the questions in order when writing their paragraph. Help reluctant writers by suggesting an opening sentence. Have students date their writing and put it in their working folders.

More Practice: *Voyager 3 Workbook* p. 28

Have students fill out copies of PCM 13.

Writing Skills Mini-Lesson: More on Complex Sentences (p. 86)

Briefly review the Unit 2 mini-lesson. Then read and discuss the introduction and the first two rules, noting the use of the comma.

Read the third rule, and have volunteers read the examples. Discuss the meanings of the other words used to introduce dependent clauses. *Because* and *since* indicate a cause-and-effect relationship between the two clauses. *Although,* like *but,* indicates a contrast or something unexpected. *If* indicates

a condition—the main clause is true under a condition defined by the dependent clause. Give additional examples for each word if necessary. Some students may not be familiar with *although.* Some may have difficulty understanding cause-and-effect relationships.

Practice Read the directions for the exercise. Read, or ask a volunteer to read, the example. Be sure students understand they are to write two sentences by combining the dependent clause from the first column with the independent clause opposite it in the second column. Ask them to work independently and then read their sentences to a partner. Have students date their work and put it in their working folders.

More Practice: *Voyager 3 Workbook* p. 29

Unit 3 Review (pp. 87–88)

Follow the process described in Unit 1. As students edit their writing, have them check that they have written and punctuated compound and complex sentences correctly. Have students date their writing and put it in their working folders.

Extending the theme: To extend the theme of "Voices for Justice," use PCM 11, activity 4. Ask students to use one of the suggestions to write about one of the "voices for justice" in the unit. Remind them to prewrite.

Have students date their writing and put it in their working folders.

More Practice: *Voyager 3 Workbook* p. 31

▶ *Final Note:* Review with students the copies of PCM 13 that they have placed in their working folders. Ask what additional help they think they need with material from the three lessons and the Writing Skills Mini-Lesson in Unit 3. Discuss possible ways of meeting those needs.

▶ Unit 4: Express Yourself

Part of Unit	Voyager 3 pages	TRG pages	Workbook pages
Overview	89	58	
Lesson 10	90 – 97	58 – 59	34 – 35
Lesson 11	98 – 105	59 – 60	36 – 37
Lesson 12	106 – 111	60 – 61	38
Writing Skills Mini-Lesson	112	61 – 62	39 – 40
Unit 4 Review	113 – 114	62	41 – 43

Student Objectives

Reading

- Read a review, a story, and a student-authored poem.
- Practice the strategies of using prior knowledge, predicting content, and using prior experience.
- Identify viewpoint; understand character, setting, and plot; and make inferences.

Writing

- Write a review, a story, and a letter.

Speaking and Listening

- Discuss, read aloud, and interview.

Word Attack and Mechanics

- Divide words into syllables.
- Review word recognition strategies.
- Fix sentence fragments.

▶ Unit 4 PCMs

PCM 3: Plot Map
PCM 5: Character Web
PCM 6: Story Frame
PCM 11: Writing Starters
PCM 13: Student Progress Tracking Sheet

▶ Personal Dictionaries and Spelling Lists

Encourage students to add words they would like to learn to their dictionaries and spelling lists during each lesson in Unit 4 (see p. 42).

Unit 4 Overview (p. 89)

The overview introduces the theme "Express Yourself." Discuss the collage of pictures that represent the three readings in the unit. Ask, *"Can you think of reasons why these people might want to express themselves? Can you imagine ways they might choose to do that?"* Read the overview together. Discuss the last question and ask students how they express themselves.

Be an Active Reader See Unit 1 notes.

Lesson 10 (pp. 90–97)

Learning Goals Discuss the learning goals.

Before You Read Read and discuss the two paragraphs and the checklist. Have students complete the checklist independently. Remind them to check *all* the items they would expect to find in a review. Tell them to look for these pieces of information as they read.

Key Words See Lesson 1 notes.

Use the Strategy Review the strategy of using prior knowledge, which was introduced in Lesson 8.

"Marian Anderson: A Tribute" Discuss the photo of Marian Anderson's 1939 Easter concert at the Lincoln Memorial. Follow one of the strategies outlined in "Working with the Reading Selections" on page 14. Be sure students use the check-ins to help them apply the strategy of using prior knowledge. Tell students that a review reflects the writer's opinion or viewpoint.

After You Read See Lesson 1 notes.

Talk About It Remind students that words are not the only way people express themselves. Guide students' discussions with these two questions: *"What did each of these people communicate? What messages did they send?"*

Extending the reading: Play a recording of Marian Anderson to help students appreciate her music. You may be able to borrow one from a library. Ask students to share their opinions about her singing and then have them brainstorm words that describe it. Write the list of words on the board.

Think About It: Identify Viewpoint To review the definition of *viewpoint,* have a volunteer read the first paragraph. Then read the second paragraph and the chart. Ask students to complete the chart and discuss their answers.

Have students answer the guided practice question independently and discuss it. Remind students that people's viewpoints are based on their backgrounds, experiences, preferences, and beliefs. This writer is a big fan of Marian Anderson. Discuss why that fact naturally influences her opinions about the documentary.

Practice Make sure students understand how to do this activity. Then have them answer the questions as independently as possible. Discuss their answers.

Extending the skill: Find a movie review in the newspaper, or videotape a movie review on TV. Read or view it with students. Ask students to determine whether the review was mainly positive or negative. Making a chart of specific likes and dislikes may help. If possible, discuss the background and viewpoint of the reviewer.

Write About It: Write a Review Have a volunteer read the first paragraph. Give students a few minutes to decide what they will review.
A. Tell students to support their viewpoint with at least two specific examples from the show, movie, or reading they chose. They should write these in the chart. Explain that it is not enough to say "it was good" or "I didn't like it," because that does not help a reader understand why.
B. Help students turn their notes into a short review. Suggest that they say, *"I liked/didn't like it because . . ."* Some students might find it helpful to write two paragraphs, one each for

positive and negative comments. Have students date their writing and put it in their working folders.

Word Work: Review of Dividing Words into Syllables Review the tips, giving additional examples from previous lessons if necessary.

Read the reminder. Demonstrate this process with a word that can be divided more than one way, such as *cooperate* or *reality.*

Post the tips and examples for reference.

Practice Follow the suggestions in Lesson 7 for handling known and unfamiliar words. Have students work independently. Discuss their answers. Encourage students to look up unknown words in a dictionary and to add those they want to learn to their personal dictionaries.

Ask students to point out words that contain a root and a suffix. Discuss any word meanings that need clarification.

More Practice: *Voyager 3 Workbook* p. 34

Have students fill out copies of PCM 13.

Lesson 11 (pp. 98–105)

Learning Goals Discuss the learning goals.

Before You Read Read or have a volunteer read the first paragraph. Locate the Persian Gulf, Iraq, and Kuwait on a map or globe. Ask students what they know about that region of the world and the Persian Gulf War.

Read the directions for the activities and have students complete them.

Key Words See Lesson 1 notes.

Use the Strategy Review the strategy of prediction that was practiced in Lessons 2, 5, and 7.

"A Soldier's Story" Discuss the picture. Follow one of the strategies outlined in "Working with the Reading Selections" on page 14. Be sure students use the check-ins to help them apply the strategy of predicting. Discuss unfamiliar vocabulary. Have students use context clues to figure out

Unit 4: Express Yourself **59** ◄

the meanings of *zero hour* (the planned time for the operation to begin) and *20:00* (read as "twenty hundred hours") *army time* (8:00 P.M.).

After You Read See Lesson 1 notes.

Talk About It Remind students that people express their emotions in different ways. Writing is one way. Ask students to discuss some other positive ways to express feelings. Make a list of students' ideas.

Extending the reading: Use PCM 11, activity 5. Discuss how Al's experience in the war changed his views. Ask students to think of an experience that changed them or someone they know. Encourage them to write about it. Help them with prewriting if necessary. For instance, they might make notes in two columns labeled "Before the Event" and "After the Event." Have students put their writing in their working folders.

Think About It: Understand Character, Setting, and Plot Read and review the definitions and the plot map.

Practice Read the directions and have students answer the first five questions independently. Read and explain the directions for question 6. After students identify which parts of the plot statements a, b, and c are, they should condense the statements and fill in the plot map. Check and discuss their answers.

Extending the skill

1. Use PCM 5. Have students work in pairs to make a character web for Al Cruz, using information from the story.
2. Explain how to write a story using the "snowball" technique. Someone begins a story by composing the first sentence, the next person continues with the second sentence, and so on. Have students write a story using this method. Go around the group more than once if necessary.

Write the story on the board and have students copy it. When the story is complete, work as a group to analyze the plot using PCM 3 or to summarize the story using PCM 6. Have students date their work and put it in their working folders.

Write About It: Write a Story Read the first paragraph.

A. Read the directions. Be sure students understand what is happening in the pictures. Ask them to number the pictures *1, 2,* and *3,* to show the order in which the events take place. If necessary, help them compose brief descriptions to write on the plot map.

B. Each story should contain at least three sentences, one for each plot element. Encourage students to add details and descriptions. Discuss why students' stories vary: people draw different conclusions, some "read a lot into the pictures," others give more details, and so on.

Word Work: Summary of Strategies for Recognizing Words Read the first paragraph, review the strategies, and give examples. For each strategy, refer to the tips from previous lessons and post examples.

Practice Read the directions and do the first column of words with students. Then allow them to complete the exercise independently. Encourage students to use the dictionary when necessary. Check and discuss their answers. Ask volunteers to explain how they figured out words and determined their meaning. Have students use some of the words they had trouble with in sentences. Write the sentences on the board. Summarize by reading the reminder at the bottom of the page.

More Practice: *Voyager 3 Workbook* p. 36

Have students fill out copies of PCM 13.

Lesson 12 (pp. 106–111)

Learning Goals Discuss the learning goals.

Before You Read Have a volunteer read the first two paragraphs and have students complete the activity independently.

Review the characteristics of a poem. Remind students of the poem "Lineage," which they read in Lesson 4. Explain that the poem in this lesson also creates a strong emotional impact and has no rhyme.

Key Words See Lesson 1 notes.

Use the Strategy Review the strategy of using prior experience practiced in Lessons 1 and 4.

"Arthur" Read the poem aloud, then do a paired reading with students. Finally, let them read the poem aloud on their own. Be sure students apply the strategy of comparing their own experience with the poet's. Remind students that if there is no comma or period at the end of a line, they should not stop.

After You Read See Lesson 1 notes.

Talk About It Be sure students support their evaluation with examples from the poem.

Extending the reading: Ask students to think of someone they feel strongly about and write the person's name at the top of a blank paper. Have them list all the words and phrases they can think of to describe how they feel about that person. Then have each student write a poem, using the words they listed. Have students date their writing and put it in their working folders.

Think About It: Make Inferences Introduce the concept by giving examples of everyday situations in which people make inferences: We infer someone is on a baseball team when we see him wearing a team uniform. We infer that a person is upset from her tone of voice.

Read and discuss the first paragraph. Explain that experienced readers use the information in the text, together with their prior knowledge and experience, to make inferences about people and events as they read. Explain that making inferences is related to drawing conclusions, which students practiced in Lesson 5, since our conclusions are often based on inferences we make.

Read and work through each guided practice activity with students. Be sure students understand that an inference must be based on something in the text. The knowledge and life experience of the reader often play a role, too, but cannot be the sole basis for the inference.

Practice Have students complete the activity independently. Discuss their answers and their basis for each inference.

Extending the skill: Model making inferences by rereading the story "A Safe Place" in Lesson 7 as a group. At appropriate points, stop and demonstrate how experienced readers make inferences. For example, in the first few paragraphs, we might infer that the other women in Clara's House are also victims of abuse. When Mick is first referred to, we can infer that he is Jane's abusive partner. Have students make other inferences and explain them.

Write About It: Write a Letter Have a volunteer read the first paragraph. Tell students that they may write a letter to an imaginary friend or to a real friend. The problem can be real or fictional.

A. Explain that working with a partner is a good way to generate ideas. Help students choose their best ideas.

B. Have students read the letter frame before writing. Then allow them to complete the letter as independently as possible, using their prewriting ideas. If students prefer, they can compose their letters using a standard letter format. Have students date their writing and put it in their working folders.

More Practice: *Voyager 3 Workbook* p. 38

Have students fill out copies of PCM 13.

Writing Skills Mini-Lesson: Fixing Sentence Fragments (p. 112)

Read the first paragraph and the examples. Explain that sentence fragments like those in the examples are usually acceptable in informal conversation. Writing, however, is different from talking, and students should write in complete sentences. Tell students they should look for sentence fragments in their writing and fix them.

Read and discuss the two methods for fixing fragments.

Practice Discuss the two example sentences. Make sure students understand why they are complete thoughts. Then have students work on their own to rewrite the remaining fragments. Go over their sentences with them to be sure each is a complete thought. Ask students to identify the subjects and verbs. Have students date their work and put it in their working folders.

More Practice: *Voyager 3 Workbook* p. 39

Unit 4 Review (pp. 113–114)

Follow the process described in Unit 1. As students edit their writing, remind them to check that they have followed all the rules in the Writing Skills section of the Reference Handbook (see *Voyager 3,* p. 126). Have students date their writing and put it in their working folders.

Extending the theme: To extend the theme "Express Yourself," ask the class to choose a problem or concern, such as crime, the need for jobs, or a local issue. Lead a discussion about the causes of the problem and possible solutions. Note important points on the board. Then help students organize these points by clustering related ideas. Next, use the group Language Experience Approach (see p. 19) to write a letter to the editor of your local newspaper. Copy students' sentences as they suggest them, and ask them to read the completed letter aloud. Have the group revise and edit the letter. Then have a volunteer copy a final draft to send to the paper.

More Practice: *Voyager 3 Workbook* p. 41

▶ *Final Note:* Review with students the copies of PCM 13 that they have placed in their working folders. Ask what additional help they think they need with material from the three lessons and the Writing Skills Mini-Lesson in Unit 4. Discuss possible ways of meeting those needs.

Skills Review (pp. 115–120)

When students have finished Unit 4, have them complete the Skills Review. Explain that this review will help them evaluate their reading and writing progress. Encourage them to evaluate their progress by checking their answers against those given on page 119. They can use the Evaluation Chart on page 120 to identify any skill areas they need to work on further. Meet with individual students to go over their results. Be sure that students complete the right side of the Student Interest Inventory on pages 6–7. Have them compare their answers to those they gave prior to beginning *Voyager 3* (see "Using the Skills Review," p. 14, and "Using the Student Interest Inventory," p. 13).

Alternative Assessment: Follow the instructions on PCM 14: Tips for Preparing a Progress Portfolio to help students evaluate the material in their working folders and assemble their Progress Portfolios. Then use PCM 15: Portfolio Conference Questionnaire to conduct an evaluation conference with each student.

Photocopy Masters

The following photocopy masters (PCMs) can be photocopied for classroom activities and homework. Here are brief suggestions for using each PCM.

▶ **PCM 1: Cursive Handwriting** When you feel that students are ready, introduce cursive handwriting. Let students trace each letter, following the direction lines. Then have them practice forming the letters on a separate sheet of lined paper.

▶ **PCM 2: Cursive Handwriting Practice** Write the practice sentences on the board in cursive. Write students' names in cursive on their PCMs if needed. Have students practice cursive by signing their names, copying the sentences, and writing anything else they choose.

▶ **PCM 3: Plot Map** Use this PCM as described in the lesson notes to give students extra practice in identifying the elements of plot in a piece of fiction.

▶ **PCM 4: Main Idea and Details Organizer** Use this PCM as described in the lesson notes to give students extra practice identifying the main idea and details of what they read.

▶ **PCM 5: Character Web** Use this PCM as described in the lesson notes to give students extra practice identifying qualities of characters.

▶ **PCM 6: Story Frame** Use this PCM as described in the lesson notes to help students summarize the setting, plot, and characters of a piece of fiction.

▶ **PCM 7: Using a Dictionary** When you feel that students are ready, use this PCM to help them understand why and how to use a dictionary.

▶ **PCM 8: Common Prefixes** Use this PCM as described in the lesson notes to help teach students common word parts.

▶ **PCM 9: Common Roots** Use this PCM as described in the lesson notes to help teach students common word parts.

▶ **PCM 10: Common Suffixes** Use this PCM as described in the lesson notes to help teach students common word parts.

▶ **PCM 11: Writing Starters** Use this PCM to help students generate ideas for writing topics, to help them start writing, or to help them structure their writing.

▶ **PCM 12: Map of the United States** Use this PCM to locate geographic areas referred to in the lessons.

▶ **PCM 13: Student Progress Tracking Sheet** Have students complete this PCM each time they finish a lesson.

▶ **PCM 14: Tips for Preparing a Progress Portfolio** Use this PCM as a guide to help students prepare their portfolios. The process of preparing a portfolio may take quite a while. Discuss each question and option with students. Encourage students to evaluate each option carefully. Have them give a reason for each choice they make. Show students PCM 15 before you schedule a portfolio conference.

▶ **PCM 15: Portfolio Conference Questionnaire** Schedule individual conferences. Discuss the questions on PCM 15. Write notes on the PCM. Emphasize the progress the student has shown, using the samples chosen for the portfolio. Put a copy of the completed PCM in the student's portfolio.

Cursive Handwriting

Cursive Handwriting Practice

Practice writing your name in cursive.

Copy these sentences in cursive.

I am going to school.

Soon I will read and write well.

My friend Bob has a very good job.

He works in New York City.

Plot Map

The **plot** is the action or series of events in a story. The plot usually has three parts:

1. The **rising action** introduces the characters in the story and tells about a problem or conflict.

2. The **climax** is the event that solves the problem, the turning point of the action. It usually occurs near the end of the story.

3. The **falling action** tells the effect of the climax. The plot draws quickly to a close.

Write the rising action, the climax, and the falling action of a story on these lines. Then fill in the plot map below.

Title: _____

1. **Rising action:** _____

_____

2. **Climax:** _____

_____

3. **Falling action:** _____

_____

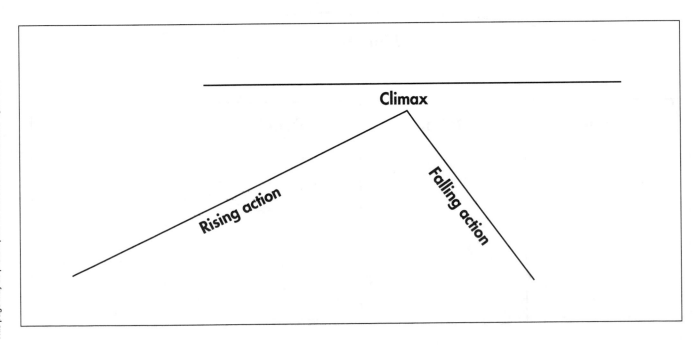

Main Idea and Details Organizer

The **main idea** of a piece of writing is the most important point that the writer wants to share.
Supporting details are pieces of information that help explain the main idea.

Write the main idea of a piece of writing in one of the diagrams below.
Then write three or four details that support the main idea.

Main Idea

Detail	Detail	Detail

Main Idea

Detail	Detail	Detail	Detail

Character Web

A **character** is a person in a story. As you read a story, you learn things about its characters. For example, you may learn

- what a character looks like
- the character's background
- what kind of person the character is
- how the character deals with life
- what the character thinks

- how the character speaks and acts
- what the character's job is
- what the character's interests are
- how the character treats others
- how others feel about the character

Fill in the details about a character you have read about on the character web below.

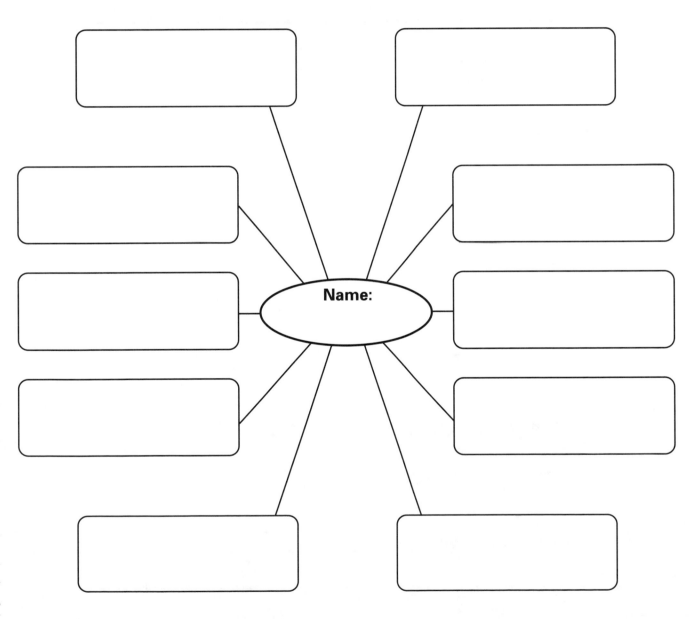

Story Frame

Title _____

The story takes place _____

_____

The main characters in the story are _____

_____

_____

The action begins when _____

_____

_____

A problem occurs when _____

_____

_____

The climax comes when _____

_____

_____

The action draws to a close when _____

_____

Using a Dictionary

Why Do People Use a Dictionary? A dictionary can tell you
- what a word means
- how a word is pronounced
- how a word is spelled
- how a word is used

The following activities will give you practice using a dictionary.

1. **Alphabetizing Review** Dictionaries list words in alphabetical order. These activities will help you review alphabetizing.

   a. Number the words in each list below in alphabetical order. You may want to write each word on an index card first and put the cards in alphabetical order.

List 1	List 2	List 3
_____ relief	_____ stomach	_____ choose
_____ quarreled	_____ special	_____ character
_____ ambulance	_____ schedule	_____ chief
_____ ceiling	_____ slight	_____ children
_____ ulcer	_____ seize	_____ change

   b. Make a list of 10 words. Write each word on an index card. Exchange cards with a partner. Alphabetize your partner's words.

2. **Getting to Know Your Dictionary**
   a. Find the first page in your dictionary that lists words starting with the letters below. Write the page number on the line next to each letter.

   B _____   E _____   G _____   J _____   M _____
   Q _____   S _____   U _____   V _____   Y _____

   b. What kind of information does your dictionary have? Look at the table of contents to see if the following sections are included. If so, write the page number on the line.

   _____ abbreviations   _____ biographical names   _____ pronunciation guide
   _____ foreign phrases   _____ geographical names   _____ signs and symbols

3. Finding Words in a Dictionary There is a pair of words in the top margin of each page in a dictionary. They are called **guide words**. The guide words are the first and last words listed on that page.

a. Use guide words to find the following words in your dictionary. Write the two guide words from the pages on the lines.

Guide Words		
_____ _____		brought
_____ _____		country
_____ _____		leisure
_____ _____		shoulder

b. The guide words on a dictionary page are **banner** and **barber**. Underline the words that would be found on that page.

barbed	barn	barbell	barbecue	bankroll
barker	banquet	bargain	barbarian	baptize

4. Reading Dictionary Entries Dictionaries may present entries in slightly different forms, but most will include the information in this sample.

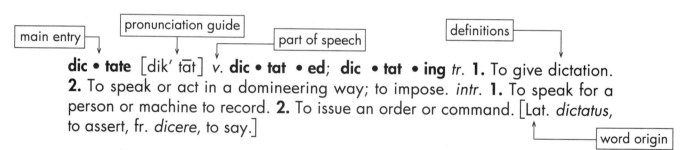

dic • tate [dik′ tāt] *v.* dic • tat • ed; dic • tat • ing *tr.* **1.** To give dictation. **2.** To speak or act in a domineering way; to impose. *intr.* **1.** To speak for a person or machine to record. **2.** To issue an order or command. [Lat. *dictatus,* to assert, fr. *dicere,* to say.]

The most important parts of a dictionary entry are usually the following:
• The **main entry** is in bold. A dot separates syllables. The word ***dictate*** has two syllables. Underline the main entry above.
• The **pronunciation** is in brackets next to the entry. Circle it. Most dictionaries use special symbols to show pronunciation. There is usually a key to the symbols on each page.
• The **definitions** explain the meanings of the word and how the word is used. Most words have more than one meaning. Each different meaning is numbered. Underline one definition with a double line.

5. Using the Dictionary Use any list or group of words to do the following activities. Look up each word and
a. write the dictionary page number
b. write the guide words on the page
c. write the pronunciation of the word
d. write one definition for the word

Common Prefixes

Prefix	Meaning	Example	Your Example
1. auto-	self	automobile	_____
*2. com-	with, together	commit	_____
con-	with, together	conform	_____
col-	with, together	collect	_____
cor-	with, together	correct	_____
*3. dis-	not	dislike	_____
dif-	not	difficult	_____
4. ex-	out of, from	exhale	_____
*5. in-	in, into	inspect	_____
im-	in, into	implant	_____
*6. in-	not	incorrect	_____
im-	not	imperfect	_____
il-	not	illegal	_____
ir-	not	irregular	_____
7. mis-	wrongly, badly	misunderstood	_____
8. post-	after	postwar	_____
9. pre-	before	prehistoric	_____
10. pro-	forth, forward	proceed	_____
11. re-	back, again	review	_____
12. sub-	under	subway	_____
13. trans-	across	transport	_____
14. un-	not, opposite of	unfriendly	_____
15. uni-	one, single	uniform	_____

*The spelling of this prefix changes according to the first letter of the root.

Common Roots

Root	Meaning	Example	Your Example
1. act	do	activate	_____
2. bio	life	biography	_____
3. cred	believe	credible	_____
4. dict	say, speak	predict	_____
*5. duce	lead	reduce	_____
duct	lead	reduction	_____
*6. flect	bend	reflection	_____
flex	bend	flexible	_____
7. form	shape	reform	_____
*8. fract	break	fraction	_____
frag	break	fragment	_____
*9. gram	write, draw	telegram	_____
graph	write, draw	graphic	_____
10. lect	gather, choose, read	elect	_____
*11. mit	send, let go	submit	_____
miss	send, let go	dismiss	_____
*12. phono	sound	phonograph	_____
phone	sound	telephone	_____
13. photo	light	photograph	_____
14. port	carry	transport	_____
*15. reg	guide, rule	regular	_____
rect	guide, rule	direct	_____
*16. scribe	write	prescribe	_____
script	write	description	_____
17. spect	watch, look at	inspect	_____
18. spire	breathe	respirator	_____
19. vent	come, arrive	convention	_____

*These roots have more than one common form.

Common Suffixes

Suffix	Meaning	Example	Your Example
*1. -able	capable	allowable	_____
-ible	capable	credible	_____
2. -al	relating to	rental	_____
*3. -ance	quality or state of	performance	_____
-ence	quality or state of	competence	_____
*4. -ant	inclined to, in a state of	expectant	_____
-ent	inclined to, in a state of	frequent	_____
5. -ant	person who	informant	_____
6. -ate	cause to, make	activate	_____
*7. -er	person who	writer	_____
-or	person who	operator	_____
8. -ian	person who	musician	_____
9. -ic	relating to	graphic	_____
10. -ion	an act, process, or condition	election, tension	_____
11. -ive	doing or tending to do	creative	_____
12. -less	without	hopeless	_____
13. -ly	in the manner of	directly	_____
14. -ment	act or condition of	measurement	_____
*15. -ty	quality	honesty	_____
-ity	quality	activity	_____
16. -ure	act, process, function	fracture	_____

*The spelling of these suffixes is determined by the root to which they are added.

Writing Starters

These writing starters can help you begin a piece of writing.

1. Write a sentence that starts with one of these.

I like . . .	Someday I will . . .
If I could . . .	I hate . . .
I hope . . .	I regret . . .
When I was . . .	I miss . . .
I believe . . .	I will never forget . . .
I once . . .	My dream is . . .

2. Complete these sentences about something you read.

The title of this reading is _____

It is about _____

I learned that _____

I think that _____

3. Respond in writing to one of these statements.
- Every cloud has a silver lining.
- Today is the first day of the rest of your life.
- A winner never quits, and a quitter never wins.
- The grass is always greener on the other side of the fence.

4. Think about a person or character you have read about. Do one of these activities.
- List questions you would like to ask the person.
- Write a letter to the person. Describe how you feel about the person's actions.
- Write about what you would have done if you had been in the person's shoes.

5. Write about an experience that has a special meaning for you.

6. Think about a decision you have made in your life. Was it wise or unwise? Write about the decision. Describe how it affected your life and others' lives.

7. Think of an incident when your beliefs or values guided your actions. Write about it. Explain how you felt about standing up for your beliefs.

Map of the United States

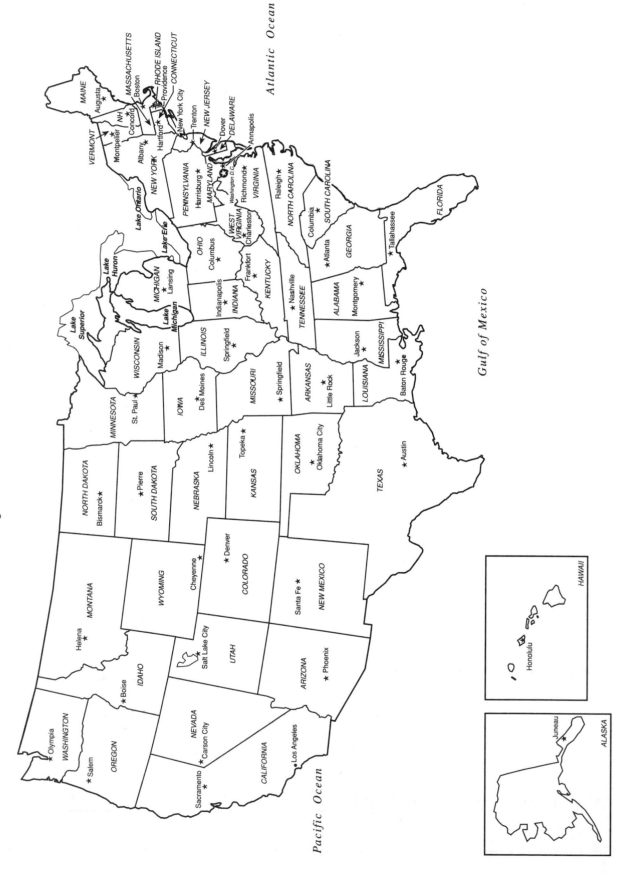

Atlantic Ocean

Pacific Ocean

Gulf of Mexico

MAINE
Augusta ★
NH
Concord ★
VERMONT
Montpelier ★
Albany ★
MASSACHUSETTS
Boston ★
RHODE ISLAND
Providence
CONNECTICUT
Hartford ★
NEW YORK
New York City
Trenton ★
NEW JERSEY
Dover ★
DELAWARE
Annapolis
PENNSYLVANIA
Harrisburg ★
MARYLAND
Washington D.C. ★
Richmond ★
VIRGINIA
Raleigh ★
NORTH CAROLINA
SOUTH CAROLINA
Columbia ★
WEST VIRGINIA
Charleston ★
GEORGIA
Atlanta ★
FLORIDA
Tallahassee ★
Lake Ontario
Lake Erie
Lake Huron
OHIO
Columbus ★
Lake Superior
Lake Michigan
MICHIGAN
Lansing ★
Indianapolis ★
INDIANA
Frankfort ★
KENTUCKY
Nashville ★
TENNESSEE
ALABAMA
Montgomery ★
WISCONSIN
Madison ★
ILLINOIS
Springfield ★
MISSISSIPPI
Jackson ★
Baton Rouge ★
LOUISIANA
MINNESOTA
St. Paul ★
IOWA
Des Moines ★
MISSOURI
Springfield ★
ARKANSAS
Little Rock ★
NORTH DAKOTA
Bismarck ★
SOUTH DAKOTA
Pierre ★
NEBRASKA
Lincoln ★
KANSAS
Topeka ★
OKLAHOMA
Oklahoma City ★
TEXAS
Austin ★
MONTANA
Helena ★
WYOMING
Cheyenne ★
COLORADO
Denver ★
NEW MEXICO
Santa Fe ★
IDAHO
Boise ★
UTAH
Salt Lake City ★
ARIZONA
Phoenix ★
WASHINGTON
Olympia ★
OREGON
Salem ★
NEVADA
Carson City ★
CALIFORNIA
Sacramento ★
Los Angeles

HAWAII
Honolulu ★

ALASKA
Juneau ★

Student Progress Tracking Sheet

Name: _____

Lesson: _____

Date started: _____ Date ended: _____

What I learned from the reading: _____

_____

_____

_____

What I learned from **Think About It**: _____

_____

_____

_____

What I learned from **Write About It**: _____

_____

_____

_____

What I liked about the lesson: _____

_____

_____

What I need more practice with: _____

_____

▶ PCM 13

Tips for Preparing a Progress Portfolio

Your Progress Portfolio will show what you have learned in the period covered by this portfolio. Follow these tips as you prepare your portfolio.

1. Photocopy your completed Student Interest Inventory. Put it in your Progress Portfolio folder.

2. Look at all the material in your working folder. Pick out the items you would like to put in your Progress Portfolio. Include all of the Student Progress Tracking Sheets that you have completed.

3. Choose the samples of your writing that you would like to put in your portfolio. Make sure your name, a title, and the date it was written are on each piece of writing.

   List the pieces of writing you picked on a separate paper. Tell why you chose each one. Put the list with the pieces of writing in your folder.

4. Think about the skills you have learned. List the skills pages you would like to put in your portfolio:

   Think About It pages:_____

   Word Work pages:_____

   Writing Skills Mini–Lesson pages:_____

   Photocopy these pages. Make sure your name and a date are on each page. Make a separate list of these pages. Put the list with the pages in your folder.

5. If you would like, photocopy pages from your Personal Dictionary and put them in your porfolio folder. Do the same for your Personal Spelling List.

6. Look through the items in your Progress Portfolio. Read the questions on PCM 15. Think about answers to these questions as you prepare for your portfolio conference.

Portfolio Conference Questionnaire

To the Instructor: Use this questionnaire as you conduct portfolio conferences with students.

Student: _____ **Date:** _____

Instructor: _____ **Course:** _____

1. Which writing samples and skills pages have you chosen for your portfolio?

2. Why did you choose these items?

3. What do these items show you that you have learned?

4. What selections are you most proud of? Why?

5. What would you like to do better?

6. What would you like to do more of?

7. What do you still need to do to reach your educational goals?